Abortion: the crisis in morals and medicine

As you did it to one of the least
of these my brethren, you did it to me.

Matthew 25:40 (RSV)

Abortion: the crisis in morals and medicine

Nigel M. de S. Cameron, M.A., B.D., Ph.D.
Warden of Rutherford House, Edinburgh

and

Pamela F. Sims, F.R.C.S., M.R.C.O.G.
Consultant in Obstetrics and Gynaecology,
Hexham, Northumberland

Inter-Varsity Press

INTER-VARSITY PRESS
38 De Montfort Street, Leicester LE1 7GP, England

First published 1986
Reprinted 1988

British Library Cataloguing in Publication Data
Cameron, Nigel M. de S.
    Abortion: the crisis in morals
    and medicine.
    1. Abortion——Religious aspects——
    Christianity
    I. Title   I. Sims, Pamela
    261.8'3   HQ767.3
    ISBN 0-85110-477-0

Set in Palatino
Typeset in Great Britain by Parker Typesetting Service,
Leicester
Printed in Great Britain by Cox & Wyman Ltd, Reading

*Inter-Varsity Press is the publishing division of the Universities
and Colleges Christian Fellowship (formerly the Inter-Varsity
Fellowship), a student movement linking Christian Unions in
universities and colleges throughout the United Kingdom and the
Republic of Ireland, and a member movement of the International
Fellowship of Evangelical Students. For information about local
and national activities write to UCCF, 38 De Montfort Street,
Leicester LE1 7GP.*

Contents

Introduction

Easy abortion is something with which we have become very familiar. In almost every country in the world it is legal in some circumstances, and in many – including our own – it is very common. Abortion is the subject of heated emotions on the part of those who favour it and those who do not. Where does the balance of the argument lie?

The strongest supporters of abortion are those who see it as an essential element in 'women's rights'. Every woman, they claim, has an absolute right to control the functions of her own body. She has a right to stop herself becoming pregnant, and if that fails she has an equal right to stop herself giving birth – so that both contraception and abortion are methods of 'birth control'. The fetus, it is alleged, is merely part of the woman's body. No-one else can challenge her right to dispose of it should she so choose.

The most public opponents of abortion have been seen as the Roman Catholic Church, and in consequence the debate about abortion has been regarded by many as a debate between a particular religious standpoint and everyone else. But this view is seriously mistaken. Opposition to abortion has come not merely from Roman Catholics but from Protestants too, and one of the most significant features of the recent development of the debate has been the public commitment of leading Evangelicals to the anti-abortion cause.

What is more, the arguments against abortion are not necessarily religious arguments at all. The famous Hippocratic Oath, which for many centuries has governed the ethics of the medical profession, was composed in ancient Greece and includes a specific prohibition of abortion. And some leading present-day opponents of abortion (such as Dr Bernard Nathanson, an American gynaecologist who once ran the largest abortion clinic in the world) make no pretence at being Christians. The essence of the case against abortion is that, before he or she is born, the child is still a child. While Christians have special reasons to believe in the sanctity of human life, they also share in the general reasons which lead every nation in the world to protect the lives of its citizens. If the life of the unborn child is in fact a human life – if the child is, right from the start, 'one of us' – then he or she is deserving of that same protection and respect which we accord to every other human life.

The extremists of the women's rights movement were, in practical terms, very influential in introducing a liberal abortion policy into Britain. Perhaps their greatest achievement has been to convince so many people who know no better that the unborn child is merely part of the mother's body. Talk of the fetus as a 'lump of jelly' and a 'collection of cells', which suggests that an abortion is basically akin to the removal of an appendix, has led many to believe that opponents of abortion are making a fuss over nothing. Yet these descriptions fly in the face of everything we know about the child before birth, as the superb photography in such books as Lennart Nilsson's *A Child is Born* has demonstrated.

How are Christians to react to this debate? Is it possible to argue that there is one 'Christian' position, or could there be several? Does the Christian have any special insight into the nature of life before birth? It is to address these questions that this book has been written. And it is because they are questions with both medical and theological dimensions that this book is the fruit of collaboration between a theologian and a gynaecologist.

Our procedure is this. First, we turn to the Bible: what does it have to say? Then we set out the way in which the church has understood the Bible's teaching in time past. Next we set out the present facts of the law and medical practice. What are the legal criteria for abortion, and how are they interpreted?

There are Christians who, sometimes with a heavy heart, defend abortion in certain circumstances. We look at some of their arguments. Then we face questions which people ask, and try to respond frankly. Finally, we look to the future and the significance of new developments in the technology of human reproduction for this debate about the life of the unborn. In the appendixes the reader is pointed to further sources of information.

Since this is a collaborative exercise we should, perhaps, indicate the extent of our individual contributions. Chapters

3, 4, 5 and 6 have been largely drafted by Pamela Sims, and 1, 2, 7 and 9 by Nigel Cameron. The answers to hard questions in chapter 8 we have framed together. But we would wish to add that we find ourselves in agreement on each of the positions taken up.

There are many people whom we would wish to thank for help not simply in the preparation of this manuscript, but for their friendship and the stimulus they have afforded us in the development of our own thinking on these grave and controversial issues. They include those who will find it impossible to agree with our conclusions. It would be invidious to name some and not others. So we would single out only our gratitude to Rutherford House, where much of the work on this project has been undertaken by us both.

This book has not been easy to write. It treats of subjects which are deeply emotive, to us and to many of those who will read it. We have written these chapters in the growing conviction that the abortion issue is no mere ethical debating-point, but rather the great question of public policy in our generation. On the way in which we approach it – and on the way in which society ultimately resolves it – must hang the respect which we maintain for all human life. The undermining of the traditions of humane medicine, traditions as old as Hippocrates and deeply undergirt in Holy Scripture, will have ultimately devastating effects upon us all.

By accepting liberal abortion the medical establishment and, with it, much Christian opinion have trespassed across the first principle of our Hippocratic tradition, that the doctor must 'do no harm', crossing the Rubicon of the sanctity of human life. With the death of every unborn child we are all diminished, as a fellow-bearer of the image of God is destroyed without just cause.

We find it impossible to forget the words of Jesus:

As you did it to one of the least of these my brethren, you did it to me (Matthew 25:40).

NIGEL M. DE S. CAMERON
PAMELA F. SIMS

1   What does the Bible say?

> For your lifeblood I will surely require a reckoning; of every
> beast I will require it and of man; of every man's brother I
> will require the life of man. Whoever sheds the blood of
> man, by man shall his blood be shed; for God made man in
> his own image.
>
> Genesis 9:5–6, RSV.

If we seek in the Bible a statement about whether or not
abortion is right, or a definition of the status of the unborn
child, we shall be disappointed. For although abortion is
not just a modern problem – it was practised in ancient
times – it is not singled out for discussion in the pages of
Scripture. Are we to take it, therefore, that – as some have
suggested – there is not a distinctively Christian view on
the subject? Can we come to our conclusions on the merits
of each individual case, without any clear biblical principles
to apply? Some Christians think that we can.

   Yet the fact that the Bible does not condemn something
in so many words does not mean that it is right for us
today. Take the example of slavery. The taking or keeping
of slaves is nowhere condemned as sinful in the Bible. Yet,
in this as in other areas, the way in which slaves are treated
and spoken of in Scripture has sown the seed of the over-
throw of the evil of slavery as an institution. The *kind* of
slavery permitted in the Old Testament (which had strict
limits), and the *way* in which Paul treats the runaway slave
in the New (telling his master that they are brothers in
Christ), speak louder than the absence of any formal prohibition. In this instance the will of God has asserted itself
from below the surface of the text of Scripture. Can the
same be said of abortion? Is this, like slavery, something
that the Bible writers accepted and allowed, but in which
we wish to go beyond them – in accordance with the will of
God which we see between the lines of the Bible pages?

The short answer is No. Abortion is not to be compared in this way with slavery. When we say that the Bible does not single out abortion for condemnation, but that it does by implication, we mean something different. How do we come to this conclusion?

ABORTION IN BIBLICAL TIMES

First, while abortion (like slavery) was widely practised in ancient times, we have good reason to believe that the Old and New Testament believing communities firmly rejected it. Unlike slavery, which was a custom accepted throughout the ancient world, abortion was hotly disputed. Not only the Jews and the Christians rejected it. An ancient Assyrian law, dating from between 1450 and 1250 BC, sentenced to death a woman who was convicted of having an abortion:

> If a woman by her own deed has cast that which is within her, and a charge has been brought and proved against her, they shall impale her and not bury her.[1]

Such a dreadful punishment indicates the seriousness with which the act was viewed by one, at least, of the neighbours of the Jews. It has sometimes been suggested that the absence of any parallel to this Assyrian law in the laws given to Israel implies that, deliberately, abortion is permitted to the Jews, and was (presumably) practised among them. But this is a strange conclusion to draw, when we consider the emphasis laid by the Old Testament on the importance of continuing the race, on the blessing which children are, and on responsibility in sexual matters. If the absence of a prohibition of abortion in the Old Testament implies that abortion is considered acceptable, then we must also assume that there were no restrictions upon it (for they are absent too). But in fact there is wide agreement that this was not so.

The Jews detested abortion, since it cut across everything they believed about the sacredness of life and the significance of begetting children. One recent author has concluded from his study of the writings of the Jews that in all the known Jewish literature up to AD 500 we have no record of an abortion which was not carried out to preserve the mother's life. So sweeping was Jewish antipathy to the practice that the Talmud, the vast collection of rabbinic teaching over hundreds of years, only once refers to an abortion for any other reason, and this is 'almost certainly' the doing of a non-Jew (it is, of course, condemned).[2] The writer continues, 'It was a given [that is, a basic assumption] of Jewish thought and life that abortion, like exposure, was unacceptable, and this was well known in the ancient world.' Such is the historical evidence that he can conclude as follows: 'Jews, unlike pagans, did not practice deliberate abortion.'[3]

We can, therefore, conclude that the Assyrian law has no parallel in the Pentateuch, since abortion was considered unthinkable. It denied so many of the convictions of the Jews that it required no condemnation.

We have clear evidence also that the Jews of Jesus' own day – from the best of whom the first Christians took over so much of their thinking – understood their Bible (the Old Testament) to forbid abortion absolutely. For example Josephus, the Jewish historian, writes as follows:

> The Law forbids women either to cause abortion or to make away with the foetus; a woman convicted of this is regarded as an infanticide . . . [that is, someone who had killed her child].[4]

The first Christians were at least equally clear in their adoption of the same position. For example, the *Didache*, a very important and very early document (which is probably from the first century, and may be earlier than parts of the New Testament) says simply: 'You shall not slay the child by abortions. You shall not kill what is generated.'[5] We look at more examples of early Christian thinking in a later chapter. In the midst of a society in which abortion was frequent, the Christians firmly resisted and opposed it.

A SPECIAL CASE OF MURDER

It is clear, then, that the Jews and the early Christian church interpreted their Scriptures to teach a prohibition of abortion. It could be said, of course, that in this way they were mistaken; that for some reason or other they read into

Scripture something which was not there, either stated or implied.[6] So we come to our second question: granted that the biblical communities, in common with some other ancient peoples, rejected abortion, were they right in coming to this conclusion? That is to say, do the biblical documents – which they took to be their authority – support their interpretations?

That is, of course, the question with which we began: if the Bible does not outlaw abortion in so many words, does it still have something to say on the subject? We have noted that those who lived in biblical times evidently thought that it had. During the period of Greek and Roman influence, from which most of our evidence dates, and when the Jews were seen to take a distinctive position, the pressures must have been strong upon them to move to an easier stance. That they refused (and even those most influenced by Greek thought, like Philo, all refused) suggests that they were firmly convinced that their Scriptures spoke against abortion. They may have been mistaken, but their testimony grants us a reasonable presumption in favour of their reading of their own Bible, the Old Testament.

The best way into this discussion is by looking again at *how* those who opposed abortion argued their case. What does Josephus say? A woman convicted of causing an abortion is guilty of 'infanticide'; that is to say, it is the same as if she had killed the child after it had been born (a very widespread ancient, and indeed modern, practice). The *Didache* is even plainer: 'You shall not *slay the child* by abortions'; abortion is slaying a child. These writers are not seeking to create some new prohibition, nor identifying a new sin, to add to those listed in the Bible. They are rather stating that the Bible *already* condemns the practice of abortion, because it condemns murder. Abortion is seen as merely a special case of the Sixth Commandment.

Why do they come to this conclusion? For this reason. Although the biblical writers do not show interest in the question of abortion as such (though there are some possible allusions in the New Testament[7]), they do speak, on many occasions, about the life of the unborn child. So, in the light of what the Bible says about the life of the unborn child in the womb, they come to the conclusion that abortion is a special case of the act condemned in the Sixth

Commandment. That is to say, if the fetus is already the boy or the girl 'it' will soon be seen to be, then the Sixth Commandment plainly applies to him or to her – not by extension, but in fact. This is the crucial question which lies behind the debate.[8]

So we ask: how does the Bible speak of the child before birth? Since it is not constructed as a systematic work of reference, we do not find abstract discussions of 'the child before birth'. What we have are a number of incidents and statements concerning particular children *in utero*. We must carefully examine these texts, because if it becomes evident that the biblical writers treat 'unborn children' as 'children of a very young age', then we have the plainest evidence that they are covered by the protection of the Sixth Commandment. We could not then conclude that the Bible fails to condemn abortion, but that, on the contrary, it condemns the taking of innocent human life in the gravest terms; and, since this condemnation covers the taking of life at every stage, it includes the taking of the life of the child before birth.

Before we turn to the biblical examples of children before birth, there are some general arguments which we need to consider. For the general way in which Scripture speaks about man is suggestive of our view on this special case of man before birth. First we have the fact that man is made in the 'image of God'. This proves a more helpful, because more biblical, way of understanding the question than, say, posing it in terms of the origins of 'personhood'. The evidence of Scripture is very plain in a number of respects:

1. Bearing the image of God is what makes man, and therefore *a* man, special. It is the biblical foundation of the rights and responsibilities of man. One who bears the divine image is created for eternity, and whatever may be his or her character, abilities, or ultimate destiny, the image-bearer is protected by God and his law.

2. The bearing of the divine image is species-specific. It is not any particular aptitude or grace in one or other of us which grants the image. It is our being man. Man *as such* bears the image of his or her Maker. This emerges clearly from the creation narrative in Genesis 1:26–27, and again in Genesis 9:6 where murder is forbidden: 'Whoever sheds the blood of man, by man shall his blood be shed; for in the

image of God has God made man.' It is to man, in contradistinction to the other kinds of animals, that the image is given. It is inherent in being man – in being *Homo sapiens* rather than *Gorilla gorilla* – that he or she is God's image-bearer. This may seem an obvious point, but it is highly relevant to the debate, since it entails this: whatever presents itself to us as *Homo sapiens*, man rather than some other species, is a bearer of the image of God. No-one would dispute that, from the moment of fertilization, the human embryo is a member of the species, a 'human being' rather than any other kind of being.[9]

3. Over against the tendency to suggest that what makes man special is some capacity on his or her part, the idea of the divine image is a relational idea; that is, it consists in *how God relates* to this creature which is called man. The Bible never defines what is meant by the image, but the giving of the image is tied to the *making* of man: 'in the image of God *has God made man*' (Genesis 9:6). That is to say, God makes man *as such* in a certain relationship to himself, and it is of course irrespective of man's desire or ability to respond in the relationship.

The second general consideration relates to the transmission of human life as Scripture understands it. It is not often noticed that the lengthy sections of the Old Testament, and to a lesser degree the New, which consist of genealogies have something very specific to say on the matter of the transmission of life. Take, for example, Matthew chapter 1, where the ancestry of Joseph is indicated. 'Abraham', we read in the New International Version, 'was the father of Isaac', which is a paraphrase of the original which the older translations literally reproduce: 'Abraham begat Isaac'. That is to say, the point at which Abraham began to have posterity was the point at which he *begat* his son. This is a distinct reference to the beginning of the life of Isaac *in utero*. Life is transmitted from father to child at the point of begetting, and of course the lengthy genealogies incorporated within the Scripture bear their own witness to this process, as the line of promise is carried on. This provides a further pointer in the direction of our argument, by its emphasis on the point of conception as the start of the life of each new member of the race.[10]

What, then, of the biblical references to particular

children before birth? Some are specific and have clear bearing on the subject before us. Others may be less so, and it has been claimed that some of the texts often cited in this context are metaphorical rather than literal, and that they cannot be given any decisive weight in this matter. We shall, therefore, approach these texts with care, and base our argument in cases where such an objection cannot be lodged. In the light of unambiguous statements those which are less clear will be seen to fall into place.

UNBORN CHILDREN IN THE BIBLE

Much the clearest and most important references to unborn children are found in the early chapters of the Gospel of Luke. It is perhaps because Luke was a doctor that he displays such an interest in these matters. What we read here about the lives of two particular unborn children, John the Baptist and Jesus, sheds much light on what is said elsewhere about others.

The Spirit in the womb

We read in Luke 1:15 the promise of the angel that John will be filled with the Holy Spirit, 'from his mother's womb', and if we read on in the chapter we find that this is to be taken literally. Elizabeth, John's mother, is six months pregnant when she is visited by Mary, who has just conceived. At the approach of Mary, bearing her son Jesus at a very early stage, John leaps in his mother's womb 'for joy' (1:41, 44). As Geldenhuys has it in the *New International Commentary*,

> When Mary salutes her, Elizabeth's unborn babe leaps for joy, through the incomprehensible working of the Spirit of God, to salute the Son of God who has been conceived in the virgin's womb by the power of that same Spirit.

This event – the rejoicing, by the power of the Spirit, of the infant John *in utero* – is perhaps the most striking of all the biblical references to the life of the unborn child. The biblical statement implies that, at the end of the second trimester of gestation, the infant John is capable of something which could only be postulated of one who is in the full sense a human person, bearing the divine image, able (in a manner appropriate to his young age) to be pressed into divine service for a distinctly spiritual purpose. We cannot profess to understand in any detail such an account. But it clearly assumes that, before he is born, John is already related to by God and acted upon by him, in the distinctly personal manner which Spirit-filling suggests. We may remark in passing that this would seem to disprove in categorical terms the strange suggestion that it is only when a baby draws its first breath that it becomes, properly speaking, 'one of us', a man.[11]

It has been pointed out that by the late stage of his gestation the unborn John was already, as we now know, capable of much of the intellectual and other activity which we associate with human persons, and that therefore to accept his being acted upon by the divine Spirit in this manner does not entail any general recognition of person-hood or full humanity of the fetus at a significantly earlier stage. At the same time, the notion that an unborn child is regarded by God as a person capable of Spirit-filled activity at this point (when, although in modern terms he was on the borderline of 'viability', in the first century he was not) has already brought our argument a decisive stage forward. It leads us to read other references to the work of God in the lives of unborn children in Scripture in something other than a metaphorical sense. With that in mind we turn to the supreme example.

The incarnation of Jesus Christ
While John leaped in the womb, his mother Elizabeth greeted Mary with the words, 'why am I so favoured, that the mother of my Lord should come to me?' (Luke 1:43). By recognizing Mary in this way (as the 'mother' of her 'Lord'), she acknowledges the unborn Jesus as her Lord already.[12] So also, when she cries 'blessed is the child you will bear!' after calling Mary 'blessed are you among women', she speaks of the *present* blessedness of the child. What is more, the word used for 'baby' throughout this narrative is the Greek word *brephos*, which does indeed mean 'baby', and the same word is used by Luke of the new-born Jesus (2:12) and the children brought to Jesus for blessing (18:15). An alternative word for fetus could have been used, but is not.

Our discussion of Mary's encounter with Elizabeth inevitably brings us to what immediately preceded it, her encounter with the angel, Gabriel. This meeting is preparatory to the great central fact of Christian theology, the incarnation – God taking human flesh upon himself, in order to suffer and to die in our place. The Apostles' Creed puts it simply: 'Jesus Christ his only Son our Lord, Who was conceived by the Holy Ghost, Born of the Virgin Mary . . . .' That is to say, the fruit of Mary's conception, when the Spirit 'came upon her' and the 'power of the Most High' 'overshadowed her', was *Jesus Christ his only Son, our Lord*. The product of conception was none other than Jesus Christ himself, and the incarnation therefore took place not in Bethlehem (though the birth of the child was the making public of what had happened in private), but as the consequence of Gabriel's visit nine months before. So, when Elizabeth addressed her as 'the mother of my Lord', she did right. Already, in the womb of Mary, the Son of God had taken flesh and blood.

Now this is an inevitable interpretation of the Gospel narrative, and it is remarkable that its implications have not generally been realized. For the point of conception is the only point at which the miracle of the incarnation could have taken place. And the weighty terms in which the virginal conception is described by the angel ('the Holy Spirit will come upon you, and the power of the Most High will overshadow you', Luke 1:35) cannot be taken to apply to anything else.[13] The text speaks of a single act by which the God-man was conceived in Mary, and the church has consistently labelled as heresy any idea that a divine 'spirit' was added to the human body of Jesus, or that somehow in some other fashion the human being that began life was mere man and was later 'adopted' to be the Son of God. The biblical stress here, as in all discussion of human generation, is on the point of *begetting* – conception itself.

This terminology of begetting is also used to describe the relations of the Son and the Father in the Godhead. So Jesus is spoken of as the 'only-begotten Son', begotten (in the words of the Nicene Creed) 'before all worlds'. To put it better, human begetting is derived from and analogous to the divine begetting of the Son by the Father in all eternity. But none of this makes sense if the point of incarnation is understood to be anything other than that of the 'begetting', the virginal conception itself. For it is here that we find the point of connection between the eternal relations of Father and Son, and their relations in the time and space of the incarnation.

The objection that Jesus' origins are different from ours will not hold, since his virginal conception is set forth as the start of a normal human experience – a normal experience on the part of God of a human life which, while free from sin and begun in miracle, is the life that all will lead. He was not spared anything that is common to man, save the personal experience of sin. It is therefore not possible to argue that he 'began' his human existence at any other point than we 'began' ours. The fertilization of Mary's ovum by the power of the Spirit which stands at the high point of the biblical narrative ('the Holy Spirit will come upon you, and the power of the Most High will overshadow you'), is the only point at which Jesus' human life could have begun.[14]

Since we have such plain evidence for the full continuity of life unborn and born in the case of John and in the supreme case of Jesus Christ, we examine other references to unborn children in Scripture with an openness to the possibility of the activity of God in their lives at this stage. We are not disappointed.

It would, of course, be possible to give a series of references at this point and to discuss them at some length. We shall not do so, because it is needful only to illustrate what has already been shown: that the biblical writers have a plain perception of the life of the unborn child as already human life, and of the continuity of their own lives after birth and before.

Jeremiah and Job curse their birth
In a striking passage, the prophet Jeremiah gives vent to his sense of dejection by wishing he had never been born. More specifically, he wishes he could have died in the womb.

> May (the LORD) hear wailing in the morning,
>   a battle cry at noon.
> For he did not kill me in the womb,

> with my mother as my grave,
>> her womb enlarged for ever.
> Why did I ever come out of the womb
>> to see trouble and sorrow
>> and to end my days in shame? (Jeremiah 20:16b–18)

This passage bears a number of plain implications, chiefly that the prophet understands his own personal existence as going back into the womb, such that, had he died *in utero*, it could be said that 'God killed *me*; not that I never was' and, conversely, since God did not kill him in the womb, he can speak of 'coming out' of the womb to see the unhappy life which has been his. The personal existence of Jeremiah is, therefore, already established before birth, and with birth it continues.

Job echoes similar sentiments. 'Why did I not perish at birth, and die as I came from the womb?' he asks (3:11). That is, he understands himself as having existed prior to that time, such that 'I' could 'die'. He later asks,

> Or why was I not hidden in the ground
>> like a stillborn child,
>> like an infant who never saw
>> the light of day? (Job 3:16)

and:

> Why then did you bring me out of the womb?
>> I wish I had died before any eye saw me.
> If only I had never come into being,
>> or had been carried straight from the womb
>> to the grave! (Job 10:18–19)

Again, the idea of his dying 'before any eye saw me' implies his personal existence prior to birth. The idea latent in the last two lines quoted is particularly interesting. Job appears to be contrasting two possibilities: that he had never come into being, on the one hand, and on the other that he had been stillborn. That is to say, the stillborn child has already come into being before it dies.

David reflects

Two famous passages in the Psalms speak in a parallel fashion. In Psalm 139 David reflects upon the making of his body *in utero*. What is striking is his persistent use of the first person:

> For you created *my* inmost being;
>   you knit *me* together in *my* mother's womb.
>   . . .
> *My* frame was not hidden from you
>   when *I* was made in the secret place.
> When *I* was woven together in the depths of the earth,
>   your eyes saw *my* unformed body. (Psalm 139:13, 15–16a)

David understands his personal existence to extend back before the processes which formed his body in the womb.

Secondly, in Psalm 51, reflecting upon his guilt, David writes that 'in sin did my mother conceive me' (v.5, RSV), that is, 'I have been a sinner . . . from the time my mother conceived me' (NIV). This verse tends to be used to illustrate something about sin and its indwelling even in the unborn child, but for our purposes it demonstrates something prior to that: the personal existence of the self, such that sin can be predicated of the unborn person. From the time of conception original sin has been present, since it is at the point of conception that the individual begins.

These three examples all confirm the understanding of the nature of the life of the fetus which is gained from reading the infancy narratives; that there is a complete continuity between life inside and life outside the womb, that the unborn child is regarded as a person, and that the moment of conception is the point at which the beginning of human life is to be found. In other words, that which constitutes a human person finds its beginning not at birth, nor at some intermediate point during pregnancy and the developing physical form of the fetus, but at the very beginning of the process. The point of conception is the moment at which there comes into existence a person who bears the image of God, who joins in the guilt of his race and who is capable even of being filled with the Holy Spirit.

A NEW LOOK AT LIFE BEFORE BIRTH

If these things are true, what may they be taken to imply? As we show in a later chapter, they are not new perceptions but rather re-statements of a view which in large measure the church has always believed. But their re-statement today is no easy thing. For the first time since its earliest years the church finds itself in a society in which abortion for all manner of causes is both legal and acceptable to the public mind. For the first time *ever* the church itself is unsure of where it stands, and Christians looking for guidance hear conflicting voices, since for the first time in the history of the world there are conscientious Christians who advocate abortion.

2 The church's view

> For the whole of Christian history until appreciably after
> 1900, so far as we can trace it, there was virtually complete
> unanimity amongst Christians . . . that, unless at the direct
> command of God, it was in all cases wrong directly to take
> innocent human life.
>
> David Braine, *Medical Ethics and Human Life*, p.11.

It is an interesting feature of current debate that both of our
national churches – the Church of England and the Church
of Scotland – have recently expressed decided opposition to
the practice of abortion in a way they have not since the
passing of the 1967 Abortion Act.[1] The general public
believes, and has been led to believe, that rejection of
abortion is something peculiar to the Roman Catholic
Church, and that Protestants are not bound by any particular view of the practice. While Roman Catholics have
been in the forefront of opposition to abortion in recent
years, they have not been there alone. In the summer of
1983, at one of the Society for the Protection of Unborn
Children's rallies in Hyde Park, the principal speaker was
billed as Mother Teresa of Calcutta. Because of her ill-health
a tape-recorded message of her greetings was played to the
thousands who were present. But there were other
speakers, and they included two whom many would see as
the most significant English-speaking Evangelicals of this
generation: John R. W. Stott and Francis A. Schaeffer. Dr
Schaeffer was known to be nearing the end of his struggle
with cancer, but had flown from the USA to be present at
the meeting. Dr Stott informed those who had gathered
that this was the first time he had ever spoken at a gath-
ering that was political in nature. That rally alone should
serve to scotch the myth that abortion is a distinctively
Roman Catholic concern.

It is a Christian concern today because it has always

been, and the witness of the first Christians was absolutely clear. As R.F.R. Gardner has it in his *Abortion: the Personal Dilemma*, 'the Church's attitude was to forbid abortion – absolutely'. Why? 'Where no-one else gave any thought to the rights of the unborn baby it was natural that these should be championed by the Church with its sense of the sanctity of life. Within the first century of its existence it had specifically condemned abortion.'[2] This reference is to the *Didache*, probably the earliest Christian document outside the New Testament; but before we examine what it says we must ask two prior questions. First, what *was* the abortion practice of the ancient world into which the church was born? It is generally the case that Christians today are in difficulty in seeking the teaching of Scripture and the mind of the first Christians on great ethical issues, since so many modern problems (such as nuclear armament) were wholly unknown in ancient times. We must tease out the possible implications of statements and principles which were directed elsewhere. Yet this is not the case with abortion, so it is important to understand the nature of the early Christians' encounter with what they saw as a great evil.

Secondly, we must examine the Jewish attitudes out of which the thinking of the first Christians grew. We have touched upon them already in chapter 1, in our discussion of the biblical position.

THE WORLD OF THE FIRST CHRISTIANS

In Greek society abortion (like infanticide by exposure) was widely practised. Both mechanical and chemical means were available from early times, and unwanted pregnancies were evidently ended by rich and poor alike, for many of the same social reasons as govern abortion today. The subject was evidently controversial, in that the famous Hippocratic Oath made physicians swear to refrain from abortion. On the other hand, both Plato and Aristotle suggested that in their ideal societies abortion would be mandatory in some circumstances, chiefly to limit family size.

A similar situation prevailed in ancient Rome. In one writer's words, 'Under the Roman Empire the practice of foeticide was carried on for reasons of poverty, sensuality, or luxury. Seneca speaks of it as practised by fashionable women in order to preserve their beauty.'[3] Some Romans appear to have resisted the practice, with the poet Ovid, for example, commenting that 'the first one who thought of detaching from the womb the fetus forming in it deserved to die by her own weapons'.[4] Hastings' *Encyclopaedia of Religion and Ethics* sums up the situation in these terms:

A broad line . . . can be drawn between barbarian, classical and Oriental ethics on the one hand and Christian on the other, with regard to the value attached to the unborn life and the rights of the individual over it.[5]

How was abortion carried out? Michael J. Gorman writes as follows:

Most common of all, according to the gynaecologist Soranos of Ephesus, were pessaries, or substances introduced directly into the womb via the birth canal. Some of these destroyed the fetus, whereas others caused its expulsion from the womb. The physician Galen wrote that certain drugs could 'destroy the embryo or rupture certain of its membranes' and lead to an abortion, perhaps alone or else by using additional chemical or physical means.

Besides using pessaries, women took oral drugs, or 'poisons' as they were frequently labeled. Medical experts of the Roman Empire, like Soranos and Dioscorides, wrote of various plant potions used as abortifacients. For example, mixtures of wine with various combinations of wallflower seed, myrtle, myrrh, white pepper or cabbage blossoms were believed to be effective in the early stages of pregnancy . . . .

Mechanical abortion techniques were often used instead of or as supplements to drugs. The crudest method, used most often by (probably desperate) women themselves, was to bind the body tightly around the womb or to strike it so as to expel the fetus. Another method required the use of abortive instruments. Two of these instruments were described by Tertullian.

The first was a 'copper needle or spike' . . . . The second tool, more sophisticated but very dangerous, required a delicate surgical operation:

Among surgeons' tools there is a certain instrument, which is formed with a nicely-adjustable flexible frame for opening the

uterus first of all, and keeping it open; it is further furnished
with an annular blade [*anulocultro*], by means of which the
limbs within the womb are dissected with anxious but unfal-
tering care; its last appendage being a blunted or covered hook,
wherewith the entire *foetus* is extracted by a violent delivery.[6]

It was into a society where these techniques were avail-
able, and where they were widely practised, that the first
Christian missions spread the gospel and established
Jewish and Gentile churches.

THE JEWS AND ABORTION

Jewish opposition to the practice of abortion was striking
and uniform. Michael Gorman can write of it in these
terms:

> Despite the absence of a specific condemnation or prohibition
> in their Scriptures, extensive research has discovered no men-
> tion of a nontherapeutic Jewish abortion in any texts of the
> Hebrew Bible or of any other Jewish literature through AD 500.
> Only a few prohibitions of abortion have been preserved in
> Jewish literature from about 150 BC. It was a given of Jewish
> thought and life that abortion, like exposure, was unacceptable,
> and this was well-known in the ancient world . . . . Though
> rare cases of abortion may have occurred in Judaism, the wit-
> ness of antiquity is that Jews, unlike pagans, did not practice
> deliberate abortion.[7]

Debate within Judaism and its different schools focused on
such questions as the appropriate penalties for abortion
and the legal standing of the fetus. There was no disagreement over the question whether abortion should be permitted 'for less than life-threatening reasons'.[8]

The failure of the Old Testament to address the question
directly was evidently interpreted by the Jews as it has
been by us (see chapter 1). As one writer has put it,

> Fœticide is not referred to in the Mosaic law. The omission is
> one indication, among many, of the intense regard felt by the
> Jewish people for parenthood and the future of their race.[9]

It is little surprise, therefore, that from the first the early Christian church adopted an uncompromising opposition to the widespread practice of abortion in the world of its day. The Jewish ethic was adopted, here as elsewhere, and became the basis for the development of distinctively Christian moral thinking.

THE EARLY CHURCH AND AFTER

We have already drawn attention to the *Didache*, the 'Teaching of the Twelve Apostles' as it is called, which dates from the earliest years of the church, and is widely believed to be contemporary with the later writings of the New Testament. In the *Didache* we read as follows: 'You shall not kill a child in the womb or murder a new-born infant.' As we have pointed out in discussing the biblical position, this identification of abortion with infanticide is characteristic: the killing of the unborn is condemned as a special case of the prohibition of all murder, not as something distinct in itself. This stems from the biblical understanding of the unborn child as someone made in the image of God.

In the second century we may note the parallel statement of the great apologist Athenagoras, in his defence of the Christians and their convictions: 'We say that those women who use drugs to bring on abortion commit murder and will have to give an account to God for abortion . . . .' Similarly, Clement of Alexandria, writing towards the end of the second century: 'But women who resort to some sort of deadly abortion drug kill not only the embryo but, along with it, all human kindness.' Other writers of the same period are:

Minucius Felix: In fact, it is among you that I see newly-born sons at times exposed to wild beasts and birds, or dispatched by the violent death of strangulation; and there are women who, by use of medical potions, destroy the nascent life in their wombs, and murder the child before they bring it forth . . . .

Tertullian: But with us murder is forbidden once and for all. We are not permitted to destroy even the foetus in the womb, as long as blood is still being drawn to form a human being. To prevent the birth of a child is to anticipate murder. It makes no difference whether one destroys a life already born or interferes with its coming to birth. One who will be a man is already one . . . .

Many other writers and important church statements could be cited, including Ambrose, Jerome, Basil the Great, John Chrysostom and Augustine. It was a universal conviction of the church that abortion, for reasons other than the defence of the mother's life, was unquestionably wrong. One study can therefore conclude in these unambiguous terms:

> For the whole of Christian history until appreciably after 1900, so far as we can trace it, there was virtually complete unanimity amongst Christians, evangelical, catholic, orthodox, that, unless at the direct command of God, it was in all cases wrong directly to take innocent human life. Abortion and infanticide were grouped together as early as the writing called the *Didache* which comes from the first century after the crucifixion. These deeds were grouped with murder in that those committing or co-operating in them were, when penitent, still excluded from Communion for ten years by early Councils . . . . The absolute war was against the deliberate taking of *innocent* life, not in the sense of sinless life, but in the sense of life which was *innocens* (not harming) . . . . We may note that this strictness constituted one of the most dramatic identifiable differences between Christian morality and pagan, Greek or Roman, morality.[10]

The pattern was set in the first centuries of the church for the following thousand years, and the moral positions taken up by influential early writers, and the legal positions enacted by the early Councils, held good throughout the Middle Ages. There was disagreement as to the severity of the legal penalty for abortion, with the view (deriving from Aristotle) gaining wide currency that before a certain stage (held to be 40 days) the embryo did not possess a soul. This led to a more lenient penalty for inducing abortion before 'animation'. Augustine, therefore, distinguished as follows:

> The embryo before it is endowed with a soul is *informatus*, and its destruction by human agency is to be punished with a fine. The *embryo formatus* is endowed with a soul; it is an animate being; its destruction is murder, and is to be punished with death.[11]

It was on this legal basis that the relatively rare occasions of abortion were dealt with during the Middle Ages. It is interesting to note that Augustine was prepared to follow through the logic of his attributions of full human person-hood to the fetus after 'animation'. So, in his *City of God*, we find him answering a question whether the fruits of abor-tion shall have a part in the resurrection of the dead. He responds, 'I fail to see why, if they are not excluded from the number of the dead, they shall not attain to the resur-rection of the dead . . . . if all human souls shall receive again the bodies which they had wherever they lived, and which they left when they died, then I do not see how I can say that even those who died in their mother's womb shall have no resurrection . . . . we must at least apply to them, if they rise again, all that we have to say of infants who have been born.'[12]

The widespread adoption of Aristotle's notion of 'anima-tion' (the giving of a soul) at a stage after that of conception requires comment. It is important to note that it did not lead to approval of the practice of abortion before anima-tion, but rather to lesser penalties for what was universally condemned as a fundamentally immoral act. This is a dis-tinction which must be emphasized. It should also be noted that Aristotle's own full-blown embryology, from which Augustine and others derived their notions of animation, was distinctive in other ways. Aristotle taught that the male embryo was animated at 40 days, the female not until 80 days. The early embryo had a 'vegetative' soul, which gave place to an 'animal' and, finally, after 40 or 80 days, to a 'rational' human soul. Aristotle's thinking, and that of those who followed him, was evidently influenced by the erroneous biology of the time, and was intended to be in harmony with it.

That is to say, what these writers attempted was to dis-cover at what stage the embryo or fetus became human (rather than, in Aristotle's terms, vegetable or animal). Once humanity could be recognized, then the full protec-tion of the Sixth Commandment (and its full penalty) was held to apply. They endeavoured to be guided by the best scientific thinking of the day as to the nature of the embryo. Embryology and the new science of genetics have made great progress since Aristotle and Augustine, and it is impossible to avoid the conclusion that the logical extension of their own principles, given the knowledge we now have about the early embryo, would be different. These two factors would be determinative: the completeness of the genetic constitution of the embryo from the point of fertilization, and the fundamental continuity in the development of the child *in utero* from that point on. The modern science of embryology does not present us with any discontinuities between 'vegetative', 'animal', or 'rational': we know now that the child *in utero* undergoes one continuous process of growth and development according to its own inner nature, determined genetically from the very start.

The first Christians' repudiation of abortion as a breach of the Commandment which forbade murder set the pattern of the church's thinking in succeeding centuries. While penalties for abortion have been various, and while medieval thought was affected by Aristotelian notions of animation, there remained a remarkable consistency until, as we have noted, 'appreciably after 1900'. So much so, indeed, that in the authoritative Hastings' *Encyclopaedia of Religion and Ethics*, which remains a standard work of reference and has stayed in print for three-quarters of a century, the writer of the article on this subject (in a volume published in 1913) can, without appearing in any way partisan, conclude by speaking of abortion of two kinds: 'the abortion which is necessary for the saving of a mother's life, and the various applications of the practice by the licentious and depraved.'

More recently, of course, many of the Protestant churches have taken up very different positions, which while continuing to stress the significance of the life of the fetus have often come to terms with abortion for reasons which would earlier have been considered unthinkable. It is difficult not to see this change of climate as the result of liberalizing tendencies in the theology of the churches, which have in many areas produced less clear-cut notions of right and wrong. The contradictory nature of the position which results is evident in many church pronouncements, which have plainly been devised to use the old words while making room for the new ideas. For example, in the fateful year of 1967 the Archbishop of Canterbury, when addressing Convocation, could speak of the 'general inviolability of the fetus' as 'normative', while going on to list the categories of possible exceptions: 'the risk of birth of a deformed or defective child; conception after rape; circumstances when the bearing and rearing of the child would prove beyond the total capacity of the mother.' Again, the Church of Scotland stated in 1966 that 'we cannot assert too strongly that the inviolability of the fetus is one of the fundamentals and its right to life must be strongly safeguarded', but then went on to add, in an almost sinister fashion, that 'we recognise that this general right is, in certain circumstances, in conflict with other rights', thus effectively torpedoing the significance of the statement of principle which had just been made. The national churches therefore offered little real opposition to the passage of the 1967 Act.[13]

IS THERE A CHRISTIAN VIEW?

So what, we may ask, is *the Christian view* of abortion? Until recent years it would not, as we have seen, have been difficult to answer that question. What began as a distinctive position over against that of Greek and Roman paganism, inherited by the first Christians from the people of God in the Old Testament, developed into the universal teaching of the church. The present acceptance of abortion, in liberal Protestantism and, indeed, in some evangelical circles, is a mark of the degree to which Christian thinking can be influenced by the pragmatism of those who have little respect for human life. Of course, present-day defenders of abortion within the Christian church vary from those who are entirely happy with the practice to others (evangelicals in particular) whose deep unease can nevertheless come to terms with what they see as sometimes a sad necessity. Yet even this position is poles apart from that of the first Christians which became the conviction of the whole church of Jesus Christ. In claiming that the church's ancient repudiation of abortion is alone biblical and fully Christian we do no more than call those modern Christians who have taken another stance back to the historic moral teaching of the church, whose origins lie in the distinctive character of the people of God in Old Testament times.

David Braine's conclusion, already quoted above, must remain before us. For the whole of Christian history, until well after 1900, there was virtually complete unanimity among Christians that abortion was the taking of innocent human life, and therefore wrong.

3 The law

. . . all in all we did not expect a very great change in practice from that obtaining before the Act. We thought there would be a slightly more liberal attitude to the problem, for that, after all, was the purpose of the new law. How wrong we were.

T. L. T. Lewis, quoted by R. F. R. Gardner in *Abortion: the Personal Dilemma*, p.75.

In 1967 the floodgates opened. With the passing of the Abortion Act that year the numbers of 'legal' operations performed per annum in the UK rose from a total of somewhere over 20,000 in 1966[1] levelling off to a staggering 160,000[2] in recent years. Put in perspective, this represents around a fifth of on-going pregnancies. Before we look more closely at the 1967 Act let us examine the provisions already existing within the framework of the law prior to that date.

PROVISIONS PRIOR TO 1967

Murder

This crime is an offence at Common Law as opposed to Statute Law. Back in the thirteenth century it was accepted opinion that it was murder to kill a child in the womb, but by the seventeenth century things had changed. Lord Coke and others agreed that murder is the unlawful killing of a 'reasonable creature in being', *i.e.* outside the womb. So what of the fetus *in utero*? It remained a serious criminal offence to destroy a human life, once its presence was made known. (As Gerard Wright, QC, points out, this law should protect the life of the tiny conceptus *in vitro*.[3])

Statute Laws have also been concerned with induced abortion. In 1803 it was made a criminal offence at any time from conception onwards and, according to a recent article,[4] 'this has been the general position since then'.

Offences Against the Person Act 1861

This law makes it an offence to administer anything to a woman to procure an abortion. Note that it is the *intent*, whether or not she is in fact pregnant, which constitutes the crime. Interest in this Act has been revived recently in discussing the post-coital pill. The Attorney General in a statement in May 1983 said that this pill was not illegal as it acted on the unimplanted fertilized egg. Central to his reasoning was the definition of 'miscarriage': he deemed that, before implantation, 'carriage' cannot have occurred. Even common sense would refute this opinion – the embryo is contained within the womb, and carried around, whether or not it is embedded in the wall of the uterus! Mr Wright comments that the word 'miscarriage' in 1861 did in fact include the expulsion of an unimplanted embryo. The post-coital pill should therefore be illegal.[5]

Infant Life (Preservation) Act 1929

This Act protects the unborn child capable of being born alive. It applies to the child still connected to its mother; once the cord is cut, and the child has an independent existence, the crime of murder comes into operation. This was seen recently concerning the 'Luton Baby'; foul play was suspected in a late abortion case, but well after the child had been separated from the mother.[6]

This Act does not attempt to predict whether or not the child has a reasonable chance of survival. It may live only a few hours afterwards, but should be alive during the process of birth. The very fact that doctors have found it necessary to administer drugs directly into the uterine cavity in cases of late abortion, to kill the baby because they fear the 'failure' of a live-birth, shows how often this Law must have been broken.

The reader may wonder about the 28-week limit. The Infant Life (Preservation) Act states that the fact that a woman has been pregnant for 28 weeks is '*prima facie* proof that the child is capable of being born alive'. It does not say that a child of less than 28 weeks' gestation is *not* capable of being born alive. This cut-off age for the fetus may have been acceptable fifty years ago, but it is well known that babies of much younger gestational age regularly survive today, thanks to modern neo-natal care.

Under the terms of the 1929 Act an offence has not been committed if the pregnancy is terminated to *save the mother's life*. Similar provision is made in the 1861 Offences Against the Person Act. Why then was there such dissatisfaction with the law as it stood? It seems that a very vocal minority persuaded the public, and Parliament eventually, that reform was necessary. The Abortion Law Reform Association (ALRA) was formed in 1936 by three women. By the mid-'60s it was a force to be reckoned with (though still with a membership of around a thousand only).

It is important to realize that the agitation of the ALRA had far more to do with the rise of the 'Women's Liberation' movement concerned with 'rights over their own bodies' than strictly medical considerations. While undoubtedly there were deaths occurring each year due to illegal ('back-street') abortions, as we shall see in chapter 5 the figures should be interpreted with care. It is extraordinary in retrospect that Parliament's response to an evil in society (for hitherto it had unquestioningly accepted that abortion was wrong) was simply to make it legal!

The Abortion Law Reform Association initially wanted abortion in three situations:

1. When it is necessary for preserving the physical or mental health of the woman.
2. When there is a serious risk of a defective child being born.
3. When the pregnancy results from a sexual offence (such as rape, incest, or intercourse with a girl under sixteen).

By 1966 a fourth had been added:

4. When the pregnant woman's capacity as a mother will be severely overstrained.

In 1938 one Aleck Bourne, a London gynaecologist, was espoused to their cause. He was prosecuted for carrying out an abortion on a 14-year-old girl who had allegedly been raped. The *Rex v. Bourne* case resulted in something of a watershed in the practice of abortion. The judge, in his summing up, was of the opinion that termination was allowable if the continuation of the pregnancy was likely to make the woman a 'physical wreck' or a 'mental wreck'. He felt that these conditions could be construed as life-threatening. On the basis of this case, for the next thirty years, gynaecologists practised abortion – depending upon their view of what constituted a 'wreck'. The most common indication for abortion became psychiatric. Harley Street psychiatrists were soon busily recommending cases to their gynaecological colleagues for termination of pregnancy. The inequality between rich and poor was inevitably exacerbated.

Interestingly, though the *Rex v. Bourne* case involved rape, when it came to drafting the bill, which was eventually passed as Law in 1967, it proved unworkable to make provision for sexual offences. From the practical point of view genuine cases of assault often do not present to the police or a doctor until well after the event. Furthermore, proof (in court) of such a crime takes time – and this the pregnant woman does not have.

A further notable fact, before we leave Aleck Bourne, is that by the end of his career we find him almost regretting his acquittal. He came to recognize its undesirable aftermath. Latterly he turns up on the executive committee of SPUC[7] (!) – but alas, the damage was done.

The Bill which eventually became Law was introduced in 1965 by David Steel. Earlier attempts had been made in 1952 and in 1961 (in the wake of the thalidomide disaster). By the mid- to late-sixties the ALRA were in full cry, organized opposition was too little and came too late. The medical profession was rather divided. Psychiatrists on the whole were rather liberal in their views, whereas gynaecologists were considerably less so. As R. F. R. Gardner says, 'many saw themselves cast in the role of executioner, there was widespread disapproval.'[8] Unfortunately that generation of gynaecologist is fast disappearing from the scene. In their place are many of a new breed: hard-liners who see abortion as a normal, admittedly rather unpleasant, aspect of gynaecological practice. A new generation has grown up on the Abortion Act of 1967 and sees little wrong with it – or even if it does, finds no easy escape. A new generation of the public (many of whom were not even born in 1967) has also grown up and it expects abortion virtually on demand.

Before we look specifically at the Abortion Act of 1967, let us remind ourselves of the high ideals traditionally held by the medical profession. In the wake of the Second World War, and mindful of the prominent role played by the medical profession in the rise of Nazism, the World Medical Organisation adopted the Declaration of Geneva in 1948. It includes the statement that 'I will maintain the utmost respect for human life *from the time of conception*'. We have seen the very considerable erosion of this standard through the piece of legislation that we are about to examine, and which is worth reading with care.

ABORTION ACT 1967
(most of it is quoted in full)

Medical termination of pregnancy

1. (1) Subject to the provisions of this section, a person shall not be guilty of an offence under the law relating to abortion when a pregnancy is terminated by a registered medical practitioner if two registered medical practitioners are of the opinion formed in good faith –

(a) that the continuance of the pregnancy would involve risk to the life of the pregnant woman, or of injury to the physical or mental health of the pregnant woman or any existing children of her family, greater than if the pregnancy were terminated; or

(b) that there is a substantial risk that if the child were born it would suffer from such physical or mental abnormalities as to be seriously handicapped.

(2) In determining whether the continuance of a pregnancy would involve such risk of injury to health as is mentioned in paragraph (a) of subsection (1) of this section, account may be taken of the pregnant woman's actual or reasonably foreseeable environment.

(3) Except as provided by subsection (4) of this section, any treatment for the termination of pregnancy must be carried out in a hospital vested in the Minister of Health or the Secretary of State under the National Health Service Acts, or in a place

for the time being approved for the purpose of this section by the said Minister or the Secretary of State.

(4) Subsection (3) of this section, and so much of subsection (1) as related to the opinion of two registered medical practitioners, shall not apply to the termination of a pregnancy by a registered medical practitioner in a case where he is of the opinion, formed in good faith, that the termination is immediately necessary to save the life or to prevent grave permanent injury to the physical or mental health of the pregnant woman.

Notification
2. (1) The Minister of Health in respect of England and Wales, and the Secretary of State in respect of Scotland, shall by statutory instrument make regulation to provide –
(a) for requiring any such opinion as is referred to in section 1. of this Act to be certified by the practitioners concerned in such form and at such time as may be prescribed by the regulations, and for requiring the preservation and disposal of certificates made for the purpose of the regulations;
(b) for requiring any registered medical practitioner who terminates a pregnancy to give notice of the termination and such other information relating to the termination as may be so prescribed;
(c) for prohibiting the disclosure, except to such persons or for such purposes as may be so prescribed, of notices given or information furnished pursuant to the regulations.

(2) The information furnished in pursuance of regulations made by virtue of paragraph (b) of subsection (1) of this section shall be notified solely to the Chief Medical Officers of the Ministry of Health and the Scottish Home and Health Department respectively.

(3) Any person who wilfully contravenes or wilfully fails to comply with the requirements of regulations under subsection (1) of this section shall be liable on summary conviction to a fine not exceeding one hundred pounds.

(4) Any statutory instrument made by virtue of this section shall be subject to annulment in pursuance of a resolution of either House of Parliament.

The third section of the Act deals with how it applies to Visiting Forces, *etc.* – basically there is the same provision.

Conscientious objection to participation in treatment

4. (1) Subject to subsection (2) of this section, no person shall be under any duty, whether by contract or by any statutory or other legal requirement, to participate in any treatment authorised by this Act to which he has a conscientious objection: Provided that in any legal proceedings the burden of proof of conscientious objection shall rest on the person claiming to rely on it.

(2) Nothing in subsection (1) of this section shall affect any duty to participate in treatment which is necessary to save the life or prevent permanent injury to the physical or mental health of a pregnant woman.

(3) In any proceedings before a court in Scotland, a statement on oath by any person to the effect that he has a conscientious objection to participating in any treatment authorised by this Act shall be sufficient evidence for the purpose of discharging the burden of proof imposed upon him by subsection (1) of this section.

Supplementary provisions. 1929 c. 34

5. (1) Nothing in this Act shall affect the provisions of the Infant Life (Preservation) Act 1929 (protecting the life of the viable foetus).

(2) For the purposes of the law relating to abortion, anything done with intent to procure the miscarriage of a woman is unlawfully done unless authorised by section 1 of this Act.

In the next section it is explained that 5.(2) above refers to the Offences Against the Person Act 1861, which we have already considered. The last sentence of the final section reads 'This Act does not extend to Northern Ireland', which still prevails today.

COMMENTS ON THE 1967 ABORTION ACT

1. Did we need this Act in the stark situation where the mother's life is in jeopardy? We have already seen that the answer is No. There was provision under existing law to perform an abortion legally to save a woman's life. It must be

stressed that truly medical indications (maternal) are exceptionally rare; when they *are* present it is obvious that if no action is taken, the net result will be the loss of both mother and fetus – as opposed to the fetus alone, if the pregnancy is aborted. There are situations when the baby needs to be delivered at a very premature stage because of a genuine medical problem, such as high blood pressure. The aim then, however, is to save both patients, if at all possible. (These matters are further discussed in chapter 8.)

2. Can this Act be interpreted as 'abortion on demand' – is not the risk of any full-term pregnancy greater than that of a first-trimester abortion? Some would argue along these lines.[9] Lawyers, T. G. A. Bowles and M. N. M. Bell, have reasoned otherwise.[10] They point out that the Act does not say that abortion is all right if *in general* it is less risky to have an early abortion than go through childbirth. It says the doctor has to consider the woman before him – is it a greater risk for *her* to go through with this pregnancy than be aborted? Statistics give an *overall* picture of mortality in childbirth. Women of all ages are included, some with pre-existing health factors such as high blood pressure. The fact is that the majority of women presenting for termination of pregnancy are young and fit, and the risk for them must be considerably less.

3. The wording of the Act is so loose that from the outset gynaecologists have brought their own interpretations to bear upon it. Whereas the adjectives 'substantial' and 'serious' are used in reference to the abnormal child, they are missing from the vitally important section 1 (1) (a). For example, in consideration of the mental health of the woman, what mother-to-be has not felt depressed at some time during her pregnancy (given the emotional turmoil which results partly from the intense hormonal changes)? Psychological factors are considered at greater length in chapter 5.

4. The clause referring to the woman's existing children is interesting. For the first time in history, we see the life of one individual (the fetus) being sacrificed, with the sanction of the law, because of the social circumstances of his siblings.

5. Two medical practitioners 'in good faith' must come to a joint agreement. In practice they are usually the referring

general practitioner and the hospital doctor to whom the woman makes her request for abortion. At least this is the case in the NHS – in the private sector patients tend to be self-referred. These two doctors sign a green-coloured form which is retained in the patient's notes. A further form is completed by the doctor performing the operation and this one is returned to the DHSS. Statistics are eventually published by the Office of Population Censuses and Surveys (OPCS). The certificates list the statutory grounds, and the doctor completing them rings the appropriate ones.[11]

It is not uncommon (certainly within the NHS) for the doctor actually performing the abortion operation never to have met the patient before. Work is often delegated in the smooth running of theatre lists. This spreads the load and, more importantly, is how junior doctors are taught. A few consultant gynaecologists do their own abortions, but the majority leave them to juniors – an abortion is considered a 'minor' case, on a par with a D & C.

6. Does the 'conscience clause' (section 4) work? Theologian David Field comments, 'Abortion laws usually contain a conscience clause for medical staff with scruples. But these are mainly ineffective. The only realistic alternatives open to a doctor who refuses to perform abortions are to get out of gynaecology or to emigrate.'[12] Refusal to do abortions certainly makes the struggle up the rungs of the career ladder more difficult, but not impossible, as one of the present writers has proved! The situation may be more difficult in fact for other hospital personnel. The effect of the 1967 Abortion Act on the medical and related professions will be discussed at greater length in chapter 5. Suffice it to say here that there *is* provision within the 1967 Act to opt out of involvement in abortions. *That right should be exercised.*[13]

7. The word 'viable' is introduced in brackets in section 5 (1). This term implies that the fetus is mature enough to make survival outside the womb a possibility. This is *not* a pre-condition of the 1929 Infant Life (Preservation) Act, as we have already seen. The 1967 Act is therefore in error.[14] Note also that there is no specific mention of 28 weeks in this Act.

Thus has the law stood since 1967. There have been attempts over the intervening years to make it tighter, particularly in the case of late abortions. As far back as 1972 a government publication on the 'Use of Fetuses and Fetal Material for Research' stated that a 'gestation of 20 weeks should be regarded as *prima facie* proof of viability at the present time'. The Lane Committee reported to Parliament in 1974 on the working of the Abortion Act.[15] It recommended an upper limit of 24 weeks and furthermore advised that infant resuscitative equipment be available in institutions where late abortions were performed. In 1975 Mr James White sponsored a Bill which would have prevented late abortions. Perhaps more notable was Mr John Corrie's Abortion (Amendment) Bill in 1979, which would have made abortions later than 20 weeks illegal. More recently there have been yet other efforts on the part of Lord Robertson of Oakridge and Mr Enoch Powell.

The Royal College of Obstetricians and Gynaecologists has always been opposed to such a change in the law, because they fear there would not be time to make the diagnosis in cases of genetic abnormality. In fact, as we shall see in the next chapter, with the recent advent of chorion biopsy in the first trimester, the present practice of genetic amniocentesis (done at around 17 weeks with a 2 or 3 week wait for the result) may become outmoded. In any event we must not forget that the majority of late abortions are done for 'social' reasons (though the overall figure for those over 20 weeks is under two per cent).

THE USA AND ELSEWHERE

We have looked at the scene as it prevails in the UK (barring Northern Ireland). What has been going on in the rest of the world? In general there has been a liberalizing of abortion laws world-wide. It is, however, perhaps worth a brief examination of the American situation, as our cultures are so closely linked.

The famous *Roe v. Wade* case in 1973 marked the start of liberal abortion in the USA. 15 million unborn children have been killed since then. The United States Supreme Court declared the right of any woman to obtain an abortion *at any stage of pregnancy*, and that Court ruling has stuck. In America they have had even greater 'problems' with live-births, since abortions are permitted as late as the woman wishes. There have been outcries from nursing staff who have witnessed the deliberate killing of aborted babies, who are sometimes a good deal more mature than the tiny, premature babies they are trying to save in the neo-natal unit.

Thinking people have not had to look far into the history of the United States to draw an analogy between the abortion mentality of today and the accepted institution of slavery in the last century. 1857 saw another famous Supreme Court ruling – the Dred Scott decision which declared that Negroes were not citizens of the United States. In the same manner that slaves were considered 'non-persons', so are unborn children today. And in America, as well as this country, the devaluing of the unborn has led to the devaluing of the newborn. Cases of blatant infanticide have cropped up on both sides of the Atlantic. Neo-nates have been starved and drugged to death because they do not measure up to the parents' or doctors' standard of normality.

President Reagan has strongly supported a return to what he calls 'American values', and they include the sanctity of human life. Recent years have seen the rise of the 'moral majority' and with influences such as the appointment of C. Everett Koop as Surgeon-General of the U.S. Public Health Service in 1982, it would seem that the climate of opinion in the States towards the unborn and defenceless must change for the better.

Let President Reagan himself close this chapter. 'Prayer and action', he writes, 'are needed to uphold the sanctity of human life. I believe it will not be possible to accomplish our work, the work of saving lives, "without being a soul of prayer". The famous British Member of Parliament, William Wilberforce, prayed with his small group of influential friends, the "Clapham Sect", for *decades* to see an end to slavery in the British empire. Wilberforce led that struggle in Parliament, unflaggingly, because he believed in the sanctity of human life.'[16]

4   Abortion in practice

It is a lonely operation. Although dilatation of the cervix, the neck of the womb, is an operation he performs many times a week, on this occasion it will be different. He takes that first dilator and is tinglingly aware that he is about to seal the fate of a fetus, that he is about to alter history. In other operations the cervix will dilate up readily, but in this operation it will fight, grip the end of the dilator and force it back into his hand. And then at last he will win, and as he does so he will wonder who has lost.

R. F. R. Gardner, *Abortion: the Personal Dilemma*, p.14.

Abortion may be defined as the loss of a pregnancy, too early for the developing baby to survive. The event may occur spontaneously, in which case it is usually referred to as 'miscarriage',[1] or it may be induced artificially. In this chapter we are going to be concerned with the methods commonly employed in what is also called 'termination of pregnancy'. Different methods apply in the different stages of pregnancy – from fertilization onwards.

INTERCEPTION METHODS OF ABORTION

The most commonly used methods of interrupting a pregnancy during its early days are not usually regarded as abortions at all: the intra-uterine (contraceptive) device (IUD or IUCD), and probably to a lesser extent the progestagen-only pill (also known as the 'mini-pill').

IUDs are made of plastic or polythene and sometimes contain copper. Their mode of action is still not completely understood.[2] The principal effect is on the endometrium (the lining of the womb) which is rendered non-receptive to the fertilized egg, preventing implantation. Furthermore, tubal motility may be altered so that there is a slowing of the passage of the developing embryo into the uterus. This would explain the relatively high incidence of ectopic pregnancy (a pregnancy developing outside the womb) known to occur in IUD users. Copper-containing devices may also exert a direct effect on the sperm themselves, preventing them from reaching the egg. It is interesting to note that in a recent paper reviewing the abortion scene in the UK, a well-known, pro-abortion gynaecologist unequivocally describes the IUD as a means of abortion (an abortifacient).[3]

The progestagen-only contraceptive pill is not to be confused with the modern, low-dose, 'combined' pill. The latter contains a mixture of the female hormones, oestrogen and a progestagen, a synthetic version of the naturally occurring hormone, progesterone. The combined pill is taken cyclically, whereas the progestagen-only pill is taken continuously. The dose of hormone in the mini-pill is very low, but it exerts its contraceptive effect through a variety of mechanisms. The chief action is thought to be upon the mucus secreted by the glands lining the cervix, the neck of the womb. This mucus is particularly important for allowing easy transfer of the sperm at the right time of the month, but provides a good barrier at other times. Under the influence of progesterone the mucus becomes thick and hostile to sperm, but should any manage to make the journey through the uterus to fertilize an egg, once again tubal motility is affected and the endometrium rendered unfavourable. The ectopic rate is as disproportionately high in those cases becoming pregnant on the progestagen-only pill, as with the IUD.

We have heard much in the media about the 'morning-after' pill and we have referred to its dubious legality in the last chapter (see page 35). The ordinary combined contraceptive pill given in larger than normal dosage and within 72 hours of unprotected sexual intercourse will prevent pregnancy by causing a possibly fertilized egg to pass out of the uterus without implanting. Similarly, a copper IUD may be inserted up to seven days after unprotected intercourse.

The arguments surrounding these post-coital means of 'contraception' are, in the view of many, rather fatuous. If the IUD is acceptable to prevent pregnancy, then why should there be such a fuss about using these same means *after* intercourse, when they function in exactly the same manner? A word of caution must be offered in response. The Offences Against the Person Act 1861 clearly states that it is the *intent* to procure an abortion that is illegal, whether or not the woman is indeed pregnant. The intention of the operator when he deliberately inserts a coil (or prescribes pills) post-coitally is arguably distinct from that of the doctor supplying contraception before sexual intercourse. The mechanism, however, and the result are undeniably the same.

Mention must be made of one more early method of abortion. 'Menstrual regulation' is the euphemistic term applied to the technique of emptying the uterus shortly after a missed period. It apparently has wider application in certain parts of the world, but in this country once again the Offences Against the Person Act should apply. A soft plastic tube is inserted into the womb attached to a syringe. When the plunger is withdrawn the negative pressure exerted produces a vacuum, which in turn sucks out the contents of the uterus. Until the fragments of tissue are examined afterwards there is no knowing whether the woman was pregnant or not; some would rather not know anyway. No anaesthetic is required and the procedure is performed on an outpatient basis. Some women's groups have even learnt to do this on themselves, and call it the 'gentle method'! Menstrual regulation, as such, is not generally available in the NHS, though many gynaecologists routinely perform a D & C at the same time as sterilization operations, just in case there is already a very early pregnancy (probably the chief cause of a 'failed' operation).

FIRST-TRIMESTER ABORTION

The vast majority of abortion operations in hospital or clinic are performed at a later stage than the above. They are broadly divided into first- and second-(or mid-) trimester terminations, the cut-off between these two groups lying somewhere between 12 and 14 weeks' gestation. The term 'fetus' will from here on be used to refer to the unborn child. Prior to 8 weeks it is an embryo, that is, essential organs such as heart or brain are still being formed. Subsequently the change is simply one of growth, and this at an incredible rate. For instance, the length of the fetus doubles from 4 inches to over 8 inches between 12 and 20 weeks. In the first trimester, abortion is safe for the woman via the vaginal route. In the second, drugs belonging to the prosta-glandin group are often used.

Over 80 per cent of abortions in England and Wales are performed during the first 12 weeks[4] and most of these are for 'social' reasons.[5] Patients may be referred to hospital via the general practitioner, or self-referred to a private clinic (about 40 per cent are NHS[6]). The choice depends upon what is available locally, the personal leanings of NHS doctors, and the desire for secrecy. Hospital admission, if only for the day, is necessary, as most operations are per-formed under general anaesthesia. Abortion cases fre-quently figure on an ordinary gynaecological list, along with the hysterectomies, 'repairs' and D & Cs. The same ward may actually contain patients undergoing investiga-tion for infertility and abortion cases in adjacent beds (though a humane Ward Sister will try to avoid this).

The operation of vacuum aspiration is the most com-monly performed type of abortion.[7] In itself it is usually straightforward, taking 5 or 10 minutes. The cervix, the neck of the womb, is dilated (as for a D & C – dilatation and curettage) by passing metal instruments of graduated diameter through its opening. The degree of dilatation required will depend on the size of the pregnancy. The fetus and placenta (afterbirth) are then removed by suction. The 'sucker' is a hollow metal or plastic instrument which is passed into the womb. It is connected to a length of plastic tubing which in turn is connected to a large glass bottle within which is created a vacuum via another attachment. Thus the contents of the uterus end up in the bottle, in bits – with a pint or so of blood. It is a gory affair.

At the present time there is much interest in so-called 'medical' methods of terminating a pregnancy. A surgical procedure is not required (nor even a doctor): the woman herself simply inserts a pessary (containing a drug of the prostaglandin group) in the vagina or takes the appropriate pills by mouth. It is claimed that such methods would relieve women of the surgical hazards of abortion. Of course, even if unrestricted use of such agents were illegal, there would soon be a brisk black-market trade.

Unfortunately (or perhaps fortunately) life is not that

simple. At present, medical methods of abortion in the first trimester are not in general usage. The main difficulty is that unless the woman is definitely in the very first few weeks of her pregnancy, abortion is usually 'incomplete', that is, portions of placenta are left behind and an operation (curettage) is necessary. Otherwise the woman is liable to continue bleeding and is susceptible to infection.

SECOND-TRIMESTER ABORTION[8]

In the private sector, abortion even beyond 20 weeks is performed in a manner similar to that described above – dilatation and evacuation (D & E). Naturally the cervix requires dilatation to a larger size, and the fetus, because it is so much bigger, has to be removed piecemeal: it could not possibly pass down the suction tube. The portion of the baby causing most difficulty for the operator is the head. The bones are much harder by this stage and a fragment of skull may easily perforate the uterine wall, with serious consequences.

Mid-trimester abortion in NHS hospitals generally involves the use of prostaglandin drugs. Prostaglandins are naturally occurring, hormone-like substances which are produced in various parts of the body, they are short-lived and act at the site of their production. Different ones are being isolated all the time, and they can now be synthetized.

Prostaglandins are available for administration in four principal forms for obstetric and gynaecological use: intravenous drip, intra-amniotic injection, extra-amniotic injection and vaginal pessary. It must be made clear that prostaglandins do not have their only application in abortion. Many an overdue obstetric patient has been the grateful recipient of a 'Prostin' pessary to start off her labour! Those same pessaries are sometimes used in early abortion cases to soften the cervix, making it easier to dilate, particularly when it is a first pregnancy in a young girl. In late termination, however, the choice usually lies between the intra- and extra-amniotic routes.

The intra-amniotic injection is made directly into the womb through the front of the abdomen. Some of the baby's water is removed, and the drug then injected. This

50

method works quickly, the patient experiences labour and delivers the fetus, often within six hours. The extra-amniotic method, on the other hand, takes longer. The drug is passed in a drip, up through a tube in the cervix, where it is deposited in the space between the bag of waters and the uterine wall. These patients may labour for up to 48 hours or even longer; otherwise the result is the same. Abortion at this gestation often results in the retention of a greater or lesser amount of the afterbirth and a D & C type of procedure is routinely performed to remove this.

Prostaglandins as such do not necessarily kill the fetus. Its immaturity, even at 20 to 22 weeks, usually results in its demise during the process of labour and delivery. This is seen in spontaneously occurring miscarriages at this relatively late stage. The further advanced the pregnancy, though, the more likely is a live birth; that is, a heartbeat, with or without breathing efforts, is present in the baby at delivery. This is an embarrassment to the abortionist and techniques have been devised to ensure that it does not happen. Concentrated salt solution (saline) or urea, injected directly into the baby's fluid, is occasionally used to kill the baby when there is a greater 'risk' that it may be born alive.

Most gynaecologists have their own arbitrary cut-off point beyond which they will not perform abortions. These days an ultrasound scan should resolve any doubts there may be concerning the dates, for gestational assessment is accurate to within a week or so. This makes cases such as the 'Luton Baby' all the more unbelievable: a child of over 30 weeks' gestation was delivered as a 'prostaglandin abortion', and not surprisingly lived![9]

Prior to the prostaglandin era, other methods of inducing mid-trimester abortion were in vogue. Hysterotomy is an operation similar to Caesarean section. The main difference is that, because of the smaller size of the uterus, it is opened in its upper portion rather than the lower, as in a later operation to save a live baby. The scar of the upper, hysterotomy, incision has the propensity to give way in any subsequent pregnancy, which made 'elective' Caesarean section preferable for further babies. Hysterotomy, in any case, was frequently combined with sterilization. The impression may be gained in the NHS that many of the late abortions are performed because of fetal abnormality. When the overall statistics are examined, however, it is seen that these account for around 15 per cent only of abortions after 20 weeks; the remainder are largely 'social'.

Saline and urea injected into the amniotic space, as mentioned above, have also been used alone to kill the fetus. Labour contractions are then stimulated with an intra-venous drip containing a drug call oxytocin. This can be used in much higher doses than at full term with a live baby. 'Nature's' response to the death of a fetus (for any reason) is for labour to supervene, sooner or later – sometimes much later. Ocytocin merely hastens the process.

Sometimes, something will go wrong in a pregnancy; the baby dies and yet is retained in the womb. When this happens early on, it is called a 'missed abortion'; if later (right up to term), it is an 'intra-uterine death'. The diagnosis can be made with certainty these days, because the absence of a heartbeat is so clearly seen on the scan. Quite apart from the feelings of the mother once she knows that her baby is dead, complications relating to the blood-clotting mechanism may rarely develop, so the decision is usually made to empty the uterus. Prostaglandins are a boon in this situation and can be used via the extra-amniotic, intra-venous, or vaginal (pessary) routes. The suction method is used in early cases.

ANTENATAL SCREENING[10]

Reference has already been made to ultrasound scanning. This has probably been the most dramatic advance in ante-natal screening over the past couple of decades. The term 'screening' implies that a whole population is surveyed, with the aim of picking up a particular problem. Antenatal care, while now accepted as a normal part of having a baby, is quite a recent phenomenon (of the last 50 years). The first challenge was to reduce maternal deaths and, later on, to reduce perinatal deaths (stillbirths plus newborn losses). Nowadays, because great strides have been made in medicine, there remains a relatively small number of babies lost for one reason or another (around 10 per 1,000 births). The causative factors in these cases are deemed 'avoidable' or 'unavoidable'.

Infections, such as syphilis in the mother, may affect the baby to a greater or lesser degree. In most units, one of the routine blood tests performed on 'booking' at the antenatal clinic checks for this. Other blood tests investigate blood antibodies, rhesus factor, immunity to German measles and so on. In areas of high immigrant population, conditions such as sickle cell anaemia are sought and may be treated during pregnancy. This demonstrates that, on the whole, screening is a good thing, helping mother and baby.

The depressing problem for Christians, opposed to taking human life at any stage, is that fairly insidiously tests have evolved which seek not to *treat* the diseased, but to *destroy*. In their enthusiasm for every child to be born healthy and 'normal', doctors have taken into their own hands the decision to abort those who in their opinion are not. The pregnant woman nowadays is faced with a barrage of investigations and some difficult decisions when she comes to the Antenatal Clinic. Having a baby today is a complicated affair.

Most worrying are the tests for spina bifida and mongolism (Down's syndrome). Spina bifida (or neural tube defect) develops in embryonic life as a failure in formation of the spine. A hollow structure, the neural tube, remains open exposing the delicate nerve tissue normally supplying the lower part of the body. This condition varies enormously in severity, the milder cases leading a completely normal life, the severest dying at birth, and many in between are helped by surgery. Spina bifida has a geographical distribution, becoming commoner further north in this hemisphere, and within Britain there are certain blackspots, such as South Wales.

The precise cause is still unknown, but recent research suggests that there may be a nutritional element. Certain studies have shown that vitamin supplements at the time of conception have significantly reduced the incidence of this distressing condition. This is all well and good for planned pregnancies, but what about the rest? Tests for spina bifida are applied to all women in some hospitals, or just to those at risk (having an affected close relative) in others.

The traditional tests for spina bifida depend on the detection of a substance called alphafetoprotein (AFP). It exudes from the surface of the spinal cord, rather like an ordinary skin burn 'weeps', and is found in the amniotic fluid and the mother's blood. Other developmental anomalies are less often the cause of a raised AFP. Interpretation of the results of tests depends on accurate gestational dating, so the woman must also have an ultra-sound scan to verify her dates. The AFP result may also be affected by factors such as a threatened miscarriage – and twin pregnancy!

Where all antenatal patients are screened, the blood test is performed first (at around 12 to 14 weeks), and any abnormal results, after rechecking, indicate amniocentesis. Where the at-risk women alone are investigated they usually proceed directly to amniocentesis at 16 to 17 weeks. The method of removing the fluid from the womb is very similar to that used for intra-amniotic prostaglandin abortion. A needle is pushed through the lower part of the abdomen straight into the uterus. It is generally performed under strict ultrasound control to avoid damage to the baby or afterbirth; even so the risk of miscarriage lies somewhere between ½ and 1 per cent. It goes without saying that the woman must understand that, should the result of her test prove abnormal, she will undergo termination of pregnancy. There is little point in carrying out a potentially hazardous investigation if its result makes no difference to the management of the case.

The test for Down's syndrome is a lengthy, costly affair. The baby's cells, after removal in the amniotic fluid sample, are grown in a special nutrient fluid, then microscopically examined during cell division. The cell nucleus contains the chromosomes, tiny strands carrying all the genetic material needed to make an entire human being. These are examined by highly trained experts in the field of genetics and a result is usually available within two or three weeks.

Down's syndrome is caused by the presence of one extra chromosome, over and above the normal number of 46. Similar syndromes are the result of portions of a chromosome missing or misplaced. Older women expecting a baby are offered amniocentesis, as the incidence of Down's in live births to women aged 35 to 39 is about 3 or 4 per 1,000, and in those aged 40 to 44 about 10 to 15 per 1,000.[11] Medical genetics facilities vary from area to area, which explains why women in one part of the country are routinely offered the investigation at the age of, say, 35, whereas it might be 39 in another.

Amniocentesis as a diagnostic tool for spina bifida may be on the wane. Ultrasound techniques are improving all the time and scanning alone will probably supersede the present invasive method of detection of neural tube defect. In addition to the more gross abnormalities, scanning can be used to diagnose less obvious ones. It is now possible to examine minutely every part of the unborn child's anatomy. In the hands of an expert even quite minor defects of the heart and urinary system, for example, may be demonstrated. This knowledge sometimes enables treatment of the baby before birth and in other cases is helpful in determining the optimal time for delivery – with paediatric surgeons on hand, if necessary.

There has been recent disquiet concerning the routine use of ultrasound scanning. Reports from America raised the possibility that its use might be linked to certain childhood cancers, deafness and abnormalities at birth. The Royal College of Obstetricians and Gynaecologists set up a working party to look at all the evidence and their conclusion is that these fears are groundless.[12] Modern machines in fact emit a very low dose of ultrasound, it is 'pulsed', with the energy output turned off 1,000 times longer than it is turned on. So an average 15-minute scan will expose the baby to ultrasound for only one second.

The positive advantages of ultrasound scanning must be stressed. First and foremost is the question of gestational dating. A significant proportion of women – even those with apparently 'certain dates' – may be wrong. If the baby does not seem to be growing too well in later pregnancy or the woman should go very overdue, it is of prime importance to know the true gestational age. One scan to measure the baby's head, in the second trimester, gives this information. Secondly, a scan tells us how many babies there are. Discovery of twins at birth can be a shock for all concerned! Thirdly, the position of the placenta (afterbirth) may be located – if it is low down on the wall of the uterus it may give rise to bleeding problems later on, though thankfully most 'low-lying' placentas tend to move out of the way (at least they appear to).

We have thus seen some positive applications of

scanning, but it cannot be denied that the technician is also on the lookout for abnormalities. Severer ones, when confirmed, would almost certainly lead to the woman being offered, even persuaded into, an abortion.

Finally, some less commonly used, but in other ways more sinister applications of antenatal diagnosis. Amniocentesis and chromosome analysis provide the sex of the baby with its result. This has been used in the management of patients in whom there is a high risk of producing a child with a 'sex-linked' disorder, such as muscular dystrophy. The fetus, if male, is aborted. There is also the practice (mainly in America) of aborting the 'wrong sex'. A perfectly normal child, simply because it is not of the sex desired by the parents, is done to death. This, in the long term, is bound to have serious demographic effects, since more females than males are aborted.

A further development has been fetoscopy. The fetoscope is a fine telescope which is inserted directly into the uterus, allowing direct visualization of the fetus. Abnormalities of limbs, face, spine are seen and those babies not measuring up to 'normal' are aborted. Fetoscopy is not generally available, nor is it likely to be, as its use demands an extra level of specialist training on the part of the operator. The technique has been developed chiefly to enable sampling of the baby's blood to diagnose a condition call thalassaemia. This blood disorder afflicts certain Mediterranean populations; it is not lethal at birth, but severely affected children usually die during childhood. The ultimate aim of fetoscopy is to kill the child before it gets even that far. (In a twin pregnancy, where only one baby is affected, they have even developed a method of 'selective fetocide'.) The advance in treatment for thalassaemia has surely been held back by such an attitude.

In the same manner that AFP screening is being replaced by better ultrasound, so it appears that amniocentesis for Down's (and other inherited disorders) will one day become a thing of the past. A technique has been developed to obtain early placental tissue by the vaginal or abdominal routes during the first two months. Fetal cells are then cultured for genetic study. This is called 'chorion biopsy'. It has been especially researched in countries such as Italy, where late abortions are illegal. In our country too, the obvious 'advantages' are that the woman is saved a mid-trimester abortion (more complicated, as seen above) and she can get on with trying again, if necessary. This test is not generally available at the time of writing.

COMPLICATIONS AND AFTER-EFFECTS OF ABORTION

Opponents of abortion have, in former years, been able to make much of these factors. But we need to be careful. Abortions done in the early '70s cannot be properly compared with those performed a decade later. Techniques have been 'improving' all the time, in an attempt to reduce the risks to the mother, both immediate and long-term. It is very difficult to make sense of the medical literature as it abounds with reports from all over the world – many drawing conclusions which tally rather with the authors' moral view on the matter of abortion than with scientific evidence. There are few 'prospective' studies; most are 'retrospective', that is they look back at hospital records, or send out questionnaires to women who have already had an abortion. To prove that abortion has the detrimental effects we suppose, a group undergoing abortion has to be exactly matched, for age, social class, marital status, number of previous pregnancies, sexual habits, contraceptive usage, smoking habits, *etc.*, with another group not having an abortion. Then one has to decide whether to compare the abortion group with women who have had a spontaneous miscarriage, a full-term pregnancy or no pregnancy at all. These groups of women may now be followed into the future. Just such a prospective study, one of the largest of its kind, was set up jointly between the Royal Colleges of General Practitioners and Obstetricians and Gynaecologists – its findings were published in 1985.[13] We shall look at the conclusions a little later in this chapter.

Immediate complications
These can be broadly divided into bleeding and infection. The pregnant uterus is an extremely vascular structure, that is, there is a much larger than normal amount of blood circulating through it. Well before the pregnant woman 'shows', her pulse rate has increased and the heart is actually putting out more blood with each beat: all this is to

accommodate the tiny fetus which is growing at a pheno-
menal rate. The wall of the womb is much softer than in the
non-pregnant state; a termination, even an early one, is not
strictly comparable with a D & C, though the same sort of
instruments are used. Bleeding at operation arises from
where the afterbirth was situated, but it may be excessive if
the wall of the uterus is damaged. This may even result in
perforation, necessitating an abdominal operation to repair
the defect, or hysterectomy in extreme cases. When the
uterus is perforated there is the risk of injury to other
structures such as loops of intestine – which would make
peritonitis likely.

Bleeding sometimes arises from the cervix which can be
particularly difficult to dilate in a first pregnancy in a young
girl. The very cases where the argument for abortion may
seem the strongest are those in whom damage to the cervix
of a permanent nature is the most likely.[14] Prostin pessaries
to soften the cervix first have already been mentioned;
another ploy, used more in America, has been to insert
'laminaria tents' (literally strips of dried seaweed!) in the
cervix, which swell up overnight and start the process of
dilatation.

Infection is probably most commonly associated with
fragments of placenta left behind in the womb. These form
an excellent culture medium. A quiescent infection is sometimes present in the fallopian tubes before operation, and
this is activated by the abortion, resulting in salpingitis
(infection in the tubes) afterwards.[15] These cases are particularly at risk of becoming infertile. Modern antibiotics
prevent the deaths of years ago, but often cannot eradicate
completely the milder sort of pelvic infection which leads to
menstrual irregularities, infertility and chronic pain in later
years.

Immediate complications, though not specific to abortion, include anaesthetic problems and these account for a
proportion of deaths.[16] The risks incurred in mid-trimester
abortion are similar to those mentioned above, with a few
extra ones associated with the use of prostaglandins and
other substances injected into the uterus. Reactions to
intra-amniotic injections are not unusual, but occasionally
they are severe enough to cause convulsions when saline is
used. Deaths have occasionally resulted from a breakdown

in the blood-clotting mechanism, where the patient bleeds
to death, and from various types of embolism (blood clot,
amniotic fluid or air gets into the circulation and causes
collapse) as well as extreme instances of trauma and
infection.

In the joint RCGP/RCOG study, mentioned above, over
6,000 women undergoing abortion (all methods) have been
followed up. They define 'early' sequelae as those
appearing within 21 days and they subdivide them into two
main groups – all morbidity (that is illness) and major
complications. There were no deaths. Ten per cent had
some morbidity attributable to the operation (such as
bleeding, damage to the cervix/uterus, post-operative infection, thromboembolic disease, psychiatric problems) and
two per cent had some form of major complication (for
instance haemorrhage requiring blood transfusion,
abdominal operation, severer type of mental breakdown,
and so on). The findings have roughly accorded with other
large series produced around the world. One unexpected,
though not surprising, result was that it is statistically safer
to have an abortion in the private sector. This is not surprising, because there we have abortion specialists 'expert'
in their trade.

Long-term complications
These are the cause of more controversy in the literature
than the immediate ones. They are broadly divided into
problems of fertility and difficulties in carrying a future
pregnancy.

Infection has already been discussed and is a potent
cause of tubal blockage in later months and years. The
passage of the egg down the fallopian tube is prevented,
resulting in the inability to conceive (hence the need for *in
vitro* fertilization, which in effect circumvents the tube).
Some reports also show a higher incidence of ectopic pregnancy after abortion. Note, however, that these problems
are more prevalent in any case in a population which is
sexually permissive.

Spontaneous abortion (first or second trimester) and
premature birth (occurring before the 37th week of pregnancy) are all said to be commoner in women who have
had a previous termination. In fact it may be that the

patient's socio-economic background is just as relevant. In the joint RCGP/RCOG study women undergoing abortion were matched with others with unplanned pregnancy but not having an abortion. These pregnancies were termed the 'index' pregnancy, the study looks at what happened to the first post-index pregnancy. No significant differences were found between the two groups. (Further information will be published in due course looking more specifically at the fate of those who had late abortions, and hopefully the incidence of involuntary infertility in the two groups.)

The comprehensive review of the literature by gynae-cologist Wendy Savage[17] suggests that a first-trimester abortion, performed by the vacuum aspiration method, does not increase the risk of a future first-trimester miscar-riage, though it is conceded that mid-trimester losses may be as much as doubled. The figures do suggest that D & C (for early terminations) and D & E (the removal piecemeal, as earlier described) are associated with greater risks to subsequent pregnancies. It is perhaps unfortunate that the RCGP/RCOG study recruited mainly patients having abor-tions in the NHS. This was inevitable, since many seeking a private operation would by-pass the general practitioner. The GPs have gathered much of the data.

One of the most difficult aspects to follow up is the psychological, and this will be dealt with at greater length in the next chapter. Deep, long-lasting depression may frequently result from abortion, which the doctors who performed the operation may never know about. The woman herself may not acknowledge it for years. There are anecdotal instances of guilt feelings surfacing at the time of Christian conversion. This is perhaps not surprising when the 'gut feeling' in most women is that abortion is wrong, yet this present generation (often the professionals) has been trying to persuade them otherwise.

5 The aftermath

Abortion does not end all the problems; often it just exchanges one set for another.

Francis A. Schaeffer, *Whatever Happened to the Human Race?*, p.36.

The agitations of the Abortion Law Reform Association culminated in the passing of the Abortion Act in 1967, which came into effect a year later. The pro-abortion position was generated in an atmosphere of emerging women's rights groups and a general decline of religion in the nation. What have been the results of liberalizing abortion? Have the promises and predictions of the abortionists been fulfilled?

MATERNAL DEATHS

The number of women dying from 'back-street' abortions was certainly a matter for concern. Gynaecologists nearer the end of their careers today can all recall horrific cases pertaining to the 'knitting needle' era. Various makeshift instruments were devised to push through the cervix in an attempt to disrupt the pregnancy. The woman may well have aborted, but common accompaniments were infection, 'retained products' (leading to continued bleeding and more infection) and injury to the womb itself. We shall never know how many illegal abortions were done before 1967, nor indeed how many have been done since. The records simply tell us about those cases which went wrong.[1] Infected cases were admitted to hospital, some were rendered permanently sterile, others died.

The fact is that the number of deaths attributable to abortion (of all types) has been steadily declining over the past three decades, thanks to more sophisticated antibiotics and an efficient blood transfusion service. This trend became apparent well before 1967, though the pro-abortionist would try and persuade us that the Abortion Act was responsible.

It was claimed in the 1960s that up to 200,000 back-street abortions took place each year. In 1966 the Royal College of Obstetricians and Gynaecologists produced a report on legalized abortion which estimated a figure in the region of 14,000, and added 'any other conclusion means that the results of criminal abortionists and of women interfering with themselves are better than those which can be produced by specialist gynaecologists terminating early pregnancies in the best hospital conditions'.[2]

ILLEGAL ABORTION

Has this really been made a thing of the past? The then Minister of Health wrote in 1970: 'There is more than a strong suspicion in Alexander Fleming House that the number of abortions very greatly exceeds the number of notifications.'[3] More recently the TUC produced a leaflet in opposition to the Corrie Abortion (Amendment) Bill in 1979, which also told women how to procure their own abortion. With the advent of more efficient 'do-it-yourself' kits this practice may well escalate.

It is often argued that a tightening of the law would result in a return to the 'back-streets' with horrific consequences in terms of women's lives and well-being. We cannot agree, for two reasons. First, as hinted above, for better or worse, abortion may soon be removed from the hands of doctors in any case. Technology is producing more 'reliable' aborti-facient drugs all the time, which could result in the surgical (hence the need for doctors) methods of abortion becoming obsolete.

The second reason is that there would seem to be two separate groups of women. R. F. R. Gardner refers to a Swedish study which looked at the result of refusal to grant an abortion in cases seeking it legally. Not more than 9% resorted to an illegal abortion, whereas the remainder went on with their pregnancy. 'This confirms the view that legal abortion is largely addressed to an entirely new clientele of women, who would never have had a criminal abortion, and would give birth to the child if the possibility of legal abortion had not existed.'[4]

'WANTEDNESS'

The claim made by the pro-abortion lobby was that every child would be 'wanted' if unwelcome pregnancies could be aborted. What we have seen in fact is a rise in the incidence of child abuse – as the abortion mentality has generally cheapened our view of life. Child abuse, or 'baby-battering', is now quoted as the fifth most frequent cause of death among children.[5] Certain mechanisms have been suggested by specialists in this area.[6]

Before we leave the question of wantedness it is worth reminding ourselves of a point which has often been made. The *pregnancy* may be unwanted – but there is no such thing as an unwanted *baby*. It is obvious that the current preoccupation with artificial fertility has been partly brought about by the lack of babies for adoption, for which the Abortion Act must bear some of the blame.

MALFORMATIONS

The abortionists argue the case for every child having the right, not only to be wanted, but also to be healthy. The 'cure' for the abnormal is to be killed. But who are they kidding? C. Everett Koop, in his vast clinical experience, has shown that the majority of children, with whatever deformity, are glad to be alive.[7] Down's syndrome children, in particular, can make a positive contribution to family life; though it is recognized that this is not always the case. No, those who advocate abortion of the handicapped – for the sake of the *child* – are in reality usually thinking of *themselves* (the parents, the taxpayer).

The effect of such selective abortion has not significantly altered the overall incidence of birth defects. Spina bifida is on the decrease – interestingly, more than could be accounted for by abortion and the use of vitamin supplements. Chromosome aberrations, on the other hand, are unaltered, in spite of increasingly vigorous attempts at prenatal diagnosis.[8] One effect of present abortion policies, on a more sinister note, is the almost inevitable slide into infanticide. A consumer attitude has developed – whether it is the desire to be pregnant, or not, as the case may be – and then the insistence on 'quality control' and normality of the 'product' at the end of nine months.

SOCIAL IMPLICATIONS

It was claimed by the pro-abortion lobby that liberalizing abortion would be the answer to all manner of social ills. We have just discussed the effect of treating unborn human life as easily expendable on our attitude to children, whether they be normal or handicapped babies. Let us now move on to marriage and the family. What is happening there?

The statistics in Appendix 1 confirm our worst fears. Liberal abortion, far from preventing illegitimacy[9] and under-age pregnancies,[10] is associated with a very different story. Since 1967 the illegitimacy rate has nearly doubled to around 15 per cent, after remaining a steady 4 to 5 per cent in earlier decades. The tendency is for these young girls (as usually they are) to keep their babies and become 'single-parent' families. The feeling commonly expressed is that 'if I've got to carry this child – then I'm not giving it away when it's born'. In these days of mass unemployment having a baby gives a girl something to do – quite apart from its often being the passport to accommodation! Pregnant women, or those with a baby, are given priority when it comes to housing. This partly explains again the non-availability of babies for adoption, and marriage has become so devalued that there is scarcely any stigma attached to the single girl who has a child illegitimately.

Abortion and freely available contraception have been part and parcel of the forces undermining the Christian ideal of marriage. Sex outside marriage (adultery) and before marriage (fornication) are commonplace. Parental discipline is being progressively eroded. We should therefore not be surprised to note the dramatic increase in the number of girls under sixteen having babies and abortions over the past few decades. The 'pill' has done nothing to check this trend; rather, it has been exacerbated.[11]

Note the fact that the vast majority of women having abortions have no other children,[12] scotching the argument that we must have abortion for the harassed mother, over-burdened with a large family. Instead the proportion of singles and 'others' steadily rises. Studies also show that there are a number of women who have abortions, simply to go away and get pregnant again, and return with yet another request for termination. (In other parts of the world, such as Eastern Europe, abortion is considered an extension of contraception.)

Abortion, once seen as the panacea for problems in marriage, as well as in the wider society, simply has not worked. Where a marriage is likely to break down it will do so, whether or not an unplanned pregnancy is aborted. Furthermore, abortion does not rid the community of homelessness and unemployment. It has even been argued that abortion has *caused* unemployment, by depriving the population of a generation of dependent children who would have otherwise created jobs![13]

PSYCHOLOGICAL ASPECTS

We saw in chapter 3 how psychiatric indications for abortion became common before the Act was passed, and we know from the statistics[14] that 'mental health' far exceeds any other statutory ground these days. This is probably because psychological symptoms can be so nebulous and easily fabricated (by doctor or patient); also a practice has evolved which is not based on adequate clinical research, even where there is thought to be a genuine problem. Difficulties arise in conducting surveys on women who have had abortions because (a) they may not feel disposed to answering the questions altogether honestly and (b) it may be too soon after the event for psychological after-effects to have surfaced. There seem to be two questions which we should try to answer:

1. *Do normal women undergoing abortion show an increased incidence of psychological problems?*
2. *Are mentally ill women helped by having an abortion?*

The ideal way to answer these questions is to conduct a study of large numbers of women undergoing abortion; these patients should be equally matched with 'controls' (that is, not having an abortion) and both groups followed up for many years. Problems then arise because unforeseen circumstances soon 'unmatch' the two groups.

We are left with rather unsatisfactory means of investigation. Problem-cases seem to present at three levels. 1. Women who seek counselling because of guilt or other feelings, sometimes many years after the abortion – they tend to use counselling agencies. 2. Women who become more acutely ill (psychotic) and are admitted to psychiatric wards. 3. Women committing suicide.

The first category, while not giving an accurate, overall incidence, nevertheless tells us what *type* of problems are encountered. A fairly recent study[15] lists the following symptoms, in order of prevalence: guilt (by far the most common reaction), anxiety, depression, sense of loss, anger, change in relationship with boyfriend, crying, feeling misled by misinformation or lack of information, deterioration of self-image, regret or remorse, nightmares, *etc., etc.* These women were telephoning a 'Pregnancy Aftermath Helpline', their age range was 15 to 55, and the time which had elapsed since the abortion ranged from 1 day to 25 years. It is difficult to be objective about such figures – they certainly do not help us to answer question 1. above.

One would think that the true incidence of post-abortive psychosis should be easier to examine. However, there are still problems in arriving at an overall figure. If the incidence of post-partum psychosis (mental illness occurring after the birth of a baby) is anything to go by, which is around 1 per 800 – 1,000, it means that to draw significant conclusions one would need a study with thousands of subjects. Smaller numbers of women have been studied and the following conclusions reached.[16] Abortion does precipitate severe mental illness, particularly in vulnerable women. The onset of the illness is similar to post-partum psychosis (6 to 12 weeks after abortion). The prognosis of post-abortion psychosis is considerably poorer than post-partum psychosis – which would argue the case for allowing the at-risk woman to continue her pregnancy to term. A small number of patients who had previously suffered post-abortion psychosis were allowed to proceed to term – 75 per cent had a normal outcome. The weight of the above evidence points to a strong 'No' to question 2. above.

Finally, we must examine the matter of suicide. Dr Sim found that in the city of Birmingham, over a 12-year period which spanned the late '50s and early '60s, there was only one case of suicide in a pregnant woman, and in her case the question of abortion was never raised. More recently John F. Murphy and Kieran O'Driscoll, in a review of over 74,000 deliveries during a decade in a country where abortion is illegal (the Republic of Ireland), found not a *single* case of suicide![17] Interestingly, a pregnant woman is less likely to commit suicide than her matched sister who is not pregnant, though once she had given birth the risk rises to average. The suicide risk appears to rise considerably in susceptible cases after abortion.[18]

Having dealt with psychological aspects of abortion above and looked at physical after-effects in chapter 4, we shall now turn our attention to the effects of abortion on the professions.

THE POSITION OF THE MEDICAL PROFESSION

Gynaecologists

As mentioned in the last chapter, gynaecologists were, on the whole, quite opposed to the Abortion Act initially: but they have now grown accustomed to it. There remain a few, however, who on grounds of conscience refuse to participate in abortion operations, except in the rare case of genuine medical indication. Some of these specialists were already in post before the Act was passed; a tiny minority have managed to get through the system since 1967 and been appointed as consultants; yet others have more recently adopted an anti-abortion position – having grown disillusioned with the Act. Perhaps the majority are so-called 'junior' doctors, not necessarily bent on a career in obstetrics and gynaecology, yet remaining true to their principles by avoiding involvement in abortions for the 6 or 12 months or so that they are in post.

It has been argued that doctors holding a strict pro-life view should not specialize in obstetrics and gynaecology.[19] Is this because the going will be tough for him (for it will be)? Or to protect the patient from him? Or perhaps, most likely, so that the gynaecological departments up and down the country may continue their abortioneering tactics in peace, without so much as the odd twinge of conscience? (Did you know that abortion is now the *third commonest operation performed on women in England and Wales*? – of *all* operations, not just gynaecological.)

It is salutary to note that there is now a demand, on the part of women who are opposed to abortion, for obstetricians and gynaecologists whom they feel they can trust; doctors who hold the same high view of life that they do; doctors who are not going to thrust unwanted pre-natal screening tests at them; doctors who are not going to be doing an abortion in the morning and delivering their baby in the afternoon. R. F. R. Gardner quotes from a letter in the *Lancet*: 'A patient struggling for life or to preserve a pregnancy expects the doctor to try, and go on trying beyond reason – and usually he does. But will he try quite as hard if he has just come from destroying a fetus? He may *think* he can keep the two functions separate in his mind, but the unconscious influence will be insidious.'[20]

One of the practical results for the gynaecologist who does not do abortions is that his contact with such cases is almost nil. In a busy outpatient session there is little point in a patient appearing before one doctor, who refuses the termination request, only to have to repeat the consultation with another, who will come to a decision which is in accord with the consultant in charge of the 'firm'. Similarly, if a consultant does not accede to the request of the patient (and usually of the general practitioner), he will soon find that he is no longer referred abortion cases. For the GP has to seek another gynaecological opinion. In the mean time the days and even weeks are ticking by, which may mean a late abortion for the patient. The consultant who does not perform abortions, in effect, places an extra load on his colleagues. Where the abortion load is great, for the sake of the rest of the genuine gynaecological workload, the abortion 'service' has occasionally been contracted out to the private sector.[21] Is that such a bad thing? It leaves NHS hospitals free to perform their proper function, and actually the full-time abortionist is probably technically better at the job than his NHS colleagues. The idea of the NHS paying abortion clinics is abhorrent to many – but the taxpayer is paying either way. For the hospitals, some sort of stand against abortion has been made. The public might even begin to realize that abortion is a social reality, not a medical one.

General practitioners
These are in a slightly different position, in some ways more difficult. Their role in counselling is particularly important. It is freely acknowledged that people these days visit their doctor in the way that they would have gone to their vicar or minister years ago. If the GP takes a hard line on abortion and refuses to see patients requesting abortion, he will miss out completely on opportunities for counselling. Similarly, if he is willing to chat with the patient, but never refers to hospital, he may find that, as in the case of the hospital consultant, he is soon not seeing abortion requests at all. This may be the stand that some doctors, indeed whole practices, prefer to take – and this can be a powerful witness in a community.

There is a compromise adopted by some general practitioners which seems not unreasonable. After chatting to the patient he may feel that some women have more of a case than others, and these he refers to the hospital gynaecologist, after explaining his own pro-life view. The stand can be maintained by the GP's refusal to sign the 'green form' which otherwise would make him one of the two doctors who 'in good faith' believe that the abortion should be done. This has caused ill-feeling at the hospital end, but there are other doctors involved with the case who will be in a position to sign.

Counsellors
These are often specially trained social workers, but nurses sometimes take on this role and doctors too, to a greater or lesser extent. Sad to say, the overwhelming majority of social workers adopt a pro-abortion position. This is probably a reflection of their training, which focuses on the plight of the underprivileged in general and 'problem families' in particular and teaches them that abortion is the answer. The young trainees themselves (and this applies to nurses and medical students) have grown up in a society which at the present time is a moral vacuum. The ideals and standards of our age have already been absorbed. The

art of counselling lies in the ability to work through a problem with the patient while yet maintaining a certain distance to enable her to come to her own decision. Alas, this is difficult for any of us.

Abortion counselling should include consideration of the medical aspects of the operation itself, the psychological trauma that the woman may experience (and even the spiritual, should the need arise). The family situation must be explored and the different ways that difficulties could be resolved. Many pro-life counsellors admit that the decision to have an abortion is very often a panic reaction on discovery of the pregnancy. When the matter is fully discussed and it is realized that there are alternatives to abortion, the final decision may be a different one.

In this chapter we are looking at the effect that the Abortion Act has had on the professions: the conscience of the social worker seems to have been particularly numbed (though thankfully there are exceptions to the rule).

Doctors, when cast in the role of counsellor, vary tremendously in their attitude. Some feel that the woman is unlikely to change her mind once she has got as far as the surgery – certainly, if she has made it to the hospital outpatients. They have grown cynical listening to only half-true tales of woe, produced to make that particular case sound so worthy of abortion. It then becomes an empirical decision whether or not too abort, based on factors such as gestation. Counselling is reduced to a very brief explanation of the operative risks – if that.

Nurses

What does the nurse do, who conscientiously objects to abortion? It seems that it would be impossible for her to opt for gynaecology, either in the operating theatre or on the ward, as a trained nurse. She would not be able to avoid caring for abortion cases along with the other patients. The harder question concerns the nurse in training, when a spell on the gynaecology ward would be mandatory. 'How is the 18-year-old pupil nurse going to cope? How can she finish her training if she is not prepared to do gynaecology? Or how is she going to fare if she refuses to deal with certain classes of patient? How could a duty roster, or even meal-breaks, be arranged when one nurse would not look after certain of the patients in the ward, patients perhaps not yet round from the anaesthetic? One's mind boggles at the kind of treatment the pupil nurse might receive at the hands of some senior nurses, and at the report of her conduct which would be entered on her training schedule.'[22]

In this chapter we have concentrated on personal and social effects of legalized abortion. But what of the unborn child? What does abortion mean in respect to his or her developing life?

6 The life of the unborn

For Thou didst form my inward parts;
Thou dist weave me in my mother's womb.
I will give thanks to Thee, for I am fearfully and
      wonderfully made;
Wonderful are Thy works,
And my soul knows it very well.
My frame was not hidden from Thee,
When I was made in secret,
And skilfully wrought in the depths of the earth.
Thine eyes have seen my unformed substance;
And in Thy book they were all written,
The days that were ordained for me,
When as yet there was not one of them.

Psalm 139:13–16 (NASB).

The development of the unborn child may be seen as a
continuous process with its starting-point at conception. In
this chapter we shall be tracing these events, but looking
first at what precedes them.

PREPARATION FOR CONCEPTION

The egg just primed for fertilization started its own existence way back, when the woman herself was *in utero*. The
human female is born with all the eggs she will ever have,
unlike the male who goes on producing sperm throughout
life. Germ cells are set aside in the embryo, in both the male
and the female, which undergo important changes before
the eventual emergence of mature eggs or sperm.

First, the number of chromosomes must be halved. Each
human cell contains 46 chromosomes. These are protein
chains bearing genes, which are dotted along their length.
They are arranged in pairs, one half derived from the
mother, the other from the father. The nucleus of each cell

of the body contains, in coded form on the genes, all the information required for making a complete human being. This ranges from the general features of *Homo sapiens* right down to individual details such as eye-colour and whether we shall develop diabetes in later life.

Ordinary cells divide by a process known as 'mitosis'; two new cells containing exactly similar chromosomes (and hence genetic material) are derived from their precursor. This is effected by duplication of each half of the chromosome pair and a rearrangement into new pairs, once again each with maternal and paternal halves. 'Meiosis' is the special type of division reserved for germ cells – it results in a cell of 23 chromosomes, so that the full number is restored on fertilization. The initial duplication is similar, but before there is any separation there is opportunity for exchange of genetic material between the opposite halves of each pair. This is called 'crossing-over' and is the second important step in the preparation of a new individual. The mixing of genes of maternal and paternal origin further ensures

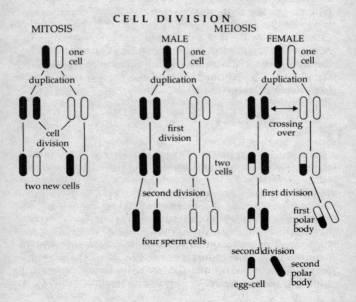

CELL DIVISION

MITOSIS   MEIOSIS

MALE   FEMALE

one cell

duplication

one cell

duplication

one cell

duplication

cell division

first division

crossing over

two new cells

second division

two cells

first division

four sperm cells

first polar body

second division

egg-cell

second polar body

uniqueness of a new being, should fertilization eventually occur.

A mature egg cell (ovum) is one of the largest found in nature, and is in fact just visible with the naked eye. Its substance is utilized by the rapidly dividing cells immediately after fertilization. The ovum achieves its size partly through unequal divisions during meiosis. Only one half resulting from each of the two divisions goes on to become the egg; the other is extruded as a blob which appears on the surface – the 'polar body'. In the case of developing spermatozoa there is no such need to preserve cytoplasm and all the genetic material is used. The four sperm thus formed contain the chromosomes neatly packaged into the head. They have a short neck and a long tail which equips them for swimming!

DETERMINATION OF SEX

The 23 chromosome pairs include the so-called sex chromosomes. This pair also derives a half from each parent: the mother always donates an X chromosome, whereas the father may contribute either an X, in which case the offspring is a girl, or a Y, making it a boy. As a result of meiosis in the male, two sperm will bear an X and the other two a Y chromosome. Interestingly, rather than the expected equal ratio of sexes at fertilization, it is more like 106:100 male to female. This compensates for the heavier loss of boys incurred through natural causes during fetal life and early childhood. However, by the time young people are themselves of reproductive age, the sex ratio is equal.

We are aware that things do go wrong from time to time, but in view of the complexity of the various mechanisms above, it is all the more remarkable that usually they go right. During crossing-over, fragments of chromosome may go missing or add themselves on to the wrong site. Separation of chromosome pairs unequally will also result in an imbalance. An extra chromosome in its entirety may turn up – a condition called trisomy, of which Down's syndrome is the commonest example. Further, the whole set of chromosomes may be over-duplicated leading to triploidy (23 is known as the haploid number in human cells, 46 the diploid number, and so on). Higher levels of ploidy are rare, but can be induced experimentally using drugs or X-rays.

The more severe the defect, the more likely it is to be lethal from the outset (as in cases of missing chromosomes and triploidy). Very minor abnormalities, however, may be undetectable in the individual unless close examination of the chromosomes is undertaken. Research has shown that among spontaneous abortuses of a very few weeks' gestation, a disproportionate number have chromosomal anomalies. No-one really knows the true rate of early pregnancy loss: some quote figures as high as 30 to 40 per cent, though recent work seems to indicate that it could well be a good deal lower.

Some would use the fact of early, natural, pregnancy loss to justify the wanton destruction (whether by abortion or experimentation *in vitro*) of what already *is* a human life which, given the right environment, is potentially viable. We answer this argument more fully in chapter 9.

FERTILIZATION AND IMPLANTATION

The egg cells are located in the ovary and, as mentioned earlier, their development starts in fetal life. At some point during the first meiotic division the whole process is arrested and held in a kind of suspended animation until the woman ovulates, releasing that particular ovum. This means that there has been an interval of nearly 50 years towards the end of reproductive life! Incidentally, this long time-interval may partly explain the incidence of chromosomal aberrations in older women. During maturation of the oocyte in the ovary, the first polar body is expelled. The second meiotic division is also suspended part way through, and indeed only completes if the egg is fertilized.

Each month, under the influence of hormones produced by the pituitary gland, egg cells start to mature. Usually just one reaches the surface of the ovary to be released from its fluid-filled vesicle, the follicle; the others shrivel up and are seen as tiny scars if an ovary is cut across. In these days of 'test tube' work drugs are given to induce 'super-ovulation' – several eggs mature at the same time and can be retrieved surgically, or under ultrasound control.

The human menstrual cycle is a complex affair involving a delicate balance of hormones. In the first 14 days up to ovulation, the oocyte is maturing and the ovary produces oestrogen in gradually rising levels. This exerts a 'feedback' effect on the pituitary which now secretes different hormones. Ovulation occurs and the ovary in the second half of the cycle puts out mainly progesterone. This latter hormone is important for its effect on the lining of the womb, the endometrium, which becomes thick and favourable for implantation, with plenty of nutriments stored by its cells.

The frond-like, outer end of the fallopian tube hovers near to the follicle as it ruptures. The egg passes into the tube and is wafted on its way towards the cavity of the womb by the action of tiny hair cells and contractions of the muscular wall of the tube itself. Fertilization occurs in the fallopian tube. Although millions of spermatozoa are released in a single ejaculate only one is required to do the job! The first on the scene penetrates the halo of small cells surrounding the ovum and then the cell membrane. Once this has happened an immediate resistance is set up to prevent entry by further sperms. The nucleus of the sperm and egg combine and cell division proceeds apace.

We cannot escape from the fact that once the sperm and the egg have combined and their nuclei fused, genetically-speaking a completely new individual has come into being. Given favourable circumstances, it will develop and grow into a full-term baby and, eventually, an adult. Geneticists and embryologists and gynaecologists all agree with this – the differences of opinion concern the *value* which we place on that new being.

Fertilization may occur up to 72 hours after sexual intercourse, The rapidly developing ball of cells then spends the next few days moving along the fallopian tube towards the uterine cavity. Nourishment at this stage is by simple diffusion from surrounding maternal fluids. By the end of the first week, however, the process of implantation begins. The tiny structure is now called a 'blastocyst' (it has a fluid-filled space within the ball of cells) and it will take several days to burrow its way into the lining of the womb. Initially the cells of the endometrium provide high energy substances such as glycogen, but soon the earliest placenta develops and the embryo derives its needs from the mother's circulation.

Implantation is occurring even before the first period is missed. These days pregnancy may be diagnosed at this early stage by measuring levels of a hormone called HCG (human chorionic gonadotrophin). This is produced by placental tissue and there are now very sensitive methods of detecting it in blood and urine. The presence of HCG forms the basis of all modern pregnancy testing. Hormonal changes in the mother's body prevent the onset of the next menstrual period, which would of course disrupt the very new pregnancy.

The normal processes of fertilization and implantation have been described; here are some deviations from the norm – some occurring naturally, other artificially.

SPECIAL CASES

Twinning
There are two basic types. Non-identical twins are easy to understand; they result from the fertilization of two separate eggs and bear no more resemblance to each other than ordinary siblings. They may be of different sex. Identical twins are a bit more complicated. They result from a single egg which at some point after fertilization develops into two embryos. The earliest possible time would be at the two cell stage, but it is more common at the beginning of the second week of development. On rare occasions this occurs even later. Examination of the membranes surrounding the babies will reveal when the division took place. The earlier the event, the more separate and complete will be each placenta and set of membranes. Identical twins are genetically exact replicas, they look alike and naturally are always of the same sex.

The problem arises for the absolutist, 'What about uniqueness now?' First, the twins *are* genetically different from anyone else and this is established at conception. Their awareness of each other as separate beings develops later.[1] Secondly, it is thought that the division into two embryos in the first place may be genetically controlled: being twins is part of their make-up. This is borne out by the hereditary element in identical twinning and its remarkably constant incidence the world round (the incidence of non-identical twins varies considerably).

Cloning[2]

This term has a sinister ring to it, with fictional visions of dozens of Hitlers or even Churchills! It implies the production of genetically identical individuals from a starter cell. In a sense, identical twins are naturally occurring clones. Animal eggs, fertilized *in vitro*, can be artificially divided into two or four, perhaps more, viable embryos, all identical.

More staggering to the lay mind is the creation of so-called 'carbon copy clones'. It is possible (only in animals so far) to take a fertilized egg, remove its nucleus and replace it with the nucleus of an ordinary cell from the adult body. The embryo which develops has the exact genetic make-up of its 'parent'. One aspect of this may well be exploited in the future – the resultant immunological compatibility. An organ becomes defunct in a patient – just grow another one in a clone!

Parthenogenesis

This is another form of reproduction, like cloning, which may be described as asexual, in that only one parent is required. It will be recalled from the description of meiosis that surplus genetic material is discarded in the form of the polar body. In some lower forms of animal life, in certain circumstances this may fertilize the egg. Some have even gone so far as to propose this mechanism for an 'immaculate' conception. This notion, with reference to the Virgin Birth, can be quashed by pointing out that all the offspring would be female, XX! Parthogenesis may be artificially induced in eggs of higher species when activated with various stimuli: chemical, temperature changes, *etc.* – the haploid number of chromosomes becomes diploid and development commences in the usual manner.

Mosaics and chimaeras

Both these types of individual have more than one type of cell in the body, from the chromosomal point of view. In mosaics two cell lines are derived from the same fertilized egg. Somehow, during very early development, perhaps through faulty separation of the chromosomes, the anomaly arises and can result in outward effects in the individual.

Chimaeras contain cell lines derived from separate fertilizations, even of different species. In the blastocyst, there appears, across the inner aspect of one pole, a layer of cells, the 'inner cell mass', which will become the embryo. During the early days it is possible to add to, or remove cells from, this mass without affecting later embryonic development. Even cells from a different species will be accepted. We have seen the horrific spectre of an animal, half sheep/half goat, through the media. What next? Half monkey/half man – trained to do menial tasks?

In vitro fertilization (IVF)
This has now become almost a household term. Scientists are able to fertilize human eggs in a glass dish in the laboratory and transfer them to the womb (embryo transfer – ET). Infertility due to blockage of the fallopian tubes may be thus overcome.

EMBRYONIC DEVELOPMENT

During the early weeks after fertilization there is an incredible amount happening all at once. Medical students groan as they attempt to take it in! We make no apology here for not being a textbook of embryology. The aim is to convey, from this brief glimpse into our earliest weeks as human beings, something of the wonder of it all.

One interesting phenomenon observed by comparative embryologists is the great similarity between early embryos of many different species, man included. Lennart Nilsson, in his beautifully illustrated book *A Child is Born*, raises the question 'When is it determined that we are going to be human beings?', and reminds us that 'This happens at the moment of conception'.[3] All the genetic information dictating how we develop – which cells differentiate into which type of tissue, and where – is encapsulated in the chromosomes of that very first cell.

The blastocyst develops the inner cell mass which becomes the 'embryonic disc'; around day 14 or 15 the 'primitive streak' appears in it, then on day 17 the 'neural groove'. Each side heaps up and by day 22 to 23 starts to fuse over, forming the 'neural tube'. Thus begins the nervous system. This tube will become the spinal cord from which nerves grow out, and one end swells to become the brain. 'Neural tube defect' (spina bifida) implies failure of fusion of the neural folds

Ethical debates surrounding the use of embryos for research have made much of the timing of events such as the first appearance of neural tissue, 'whether the embryo can feel' or the presence of recordable brain waves (at about 6 weeks). In reality these endless discussions have no bearing on the basic issues at stake – namely the individual humanity of the developing embryo from the moment of conception, whatever it looks like or can feel!

The *embryo of 4 weeks* (now 6 weeks from the mother's last period) measures about 6–7 mm and has a distinguishable head, trunk and tail. Limb 'buds' have grown out from its sides and the back has a segmented appearance. The head is much bigger than the body and as yet the face does not look at all human. There is a primitive gut connected to a structure called the yolk sac; this provides nourishment for embryos such as the chick, but in man its chief function is to manufacture blood cells. Blood is pumped around the beginnings of a circulation by a heart which initially has a single chamber.

The *embryo at 6 weeks* is about 1.5 cm long and is growing at the amazing rate of 1 mm a day. Distinctly human features are now emerging. The upper limb buds produce recognizable 'hands' at the end of very short arms (at this point the drug thalidomide caused its devastating effects); the upper limbs always develop ahead of the lower. The head is still very big compared to the body – there is plenty of activity within! Eyes and ears make their first appearance, the former first show as pigmented circles, the latter as a raised semicircle of skin somewhere in the neck region on each side. The brain, because its growth is overtaking everything else, doubles over forming the forerunners of cerebrum and cerebellum. The face is complicated. Processes grow from above and in from each side to make up the nose and jaws, including the lips and palate. Failure of fusion here results in cleft palate and/or (hare-)lip.

The yolk sac is still present at 6 weeks, but gradually the liver grows and takes over the production of blood cells.

The liver is another structure which, like the head, remains relatively large throughout fetal life and on into childhood. There are now four chambers present in the heart and the vascular system continues developing. Embryo and yolk sac are suspended in amniotic fluid, and connected by the umbilical cord to the placenta which throughout pregnancy provides nourishment for the baby and removes waste products. This is achieved by a close association between mother's and baby's circulations (without actually mixing) and diffusion of substances across the intervening gap.

The *8 week embryo* has established all the major systems. It is now called a fetus. While in the early days and weeks it has been easier to discuss the age of the embryo with reference to fertilization, from here we will speak of pregnancy as dated from the onset of the last menstrual period (adding on two weeks).

FETAL DEVELOPMENT

At 12 weeks the fetus clearly looks human. Although the mother-to-be will not have felt anything yet, it is moving its arms and legs vigorously, grimacing and even learning to suck its thumb! The tiny baby is around two inches in length and weighs under an ounce. Nerve reflexes which will equip the newborn to survive outside the womb during its first days and weeks are already developing *in utero*; turning the head in the 'searching' reflex, sucking and swallowing. Amniotic fluid passing down into the stomach is absorbed and immature kidneys produce urine. Sexual differentiation commences a little earlier than this; embryos of both sexes look alike at first, but by 12 weeks the external genitals are obviously male or female. (In passing, even at birth a cursory glance at the genitalia of a chubby baby can lead to the wrong conclusion – boys and girls occasionally appear quite similar!)

We have seen the major systems develop; now smaller details are added. Even at 12 weeks the unborn child is growing finger nails and his or her very own set of fingerprints appear! These unique patterns will remain for life. The eyes have formed and the eyelids close at this stage, not to open again until around 26 weeks' gestation. Fused eyelids used to be held as a sign of prematurity so extreme as to preclude survival – these days this is not the case.

Internally, the liver produces different types of blood cells and the fetus starts making its own antibodies to develop 'immunological competence'. The heart valves are now fully functional (though certain by-passes in the heart and lungs exist until the baby is born and takes its first breath). The skeleton of the 12 week fetus is made of cartilage; this is gradually replaced by bone in a process known as ossification. In the skull, however, the brain is initially protected by tough membrane which later turns into bone. There is a wonderful mechanism (called 'moulding') that allows alteration of the shape of the skull during birth – the bones overlap at their junctions because they have not completely fused. The 'soft spot' on top of a baby's head, where four of the bones meet, does not disappear until about 18 months of age.

Many women have an ultrasound scan at some stage of pregnancy. This technique has truly made a 'window' into the womb. Most of the facts of early human development have been gained through the study of babies lost naturally in miscarriages. The arrival of ultrasound scanning heralded a whole new era of living, dynamic pictures of the unborn child. Women may 'bond' with their infant when they first see it leaping about in the womb on the scan. Girls sometimes change their minds about abortion when they see with their own eyes that – yes, it really is a proper little baby, although perhaps not even three months yet!

Scanning (and, less commonly, fetoscopy, which gives a direct view of the baby) are dealt with in more detail in chapter 4. Let us here be thankful for some of the positive aspects of technology – the joy on a mother's face as we see tiny fingers moving across the screen, as little feet thump against the side of the womb: these may be as yet unfelt.

Doctors these days do not seem to take much notice of 'quickening', that special date when a mother first feels her baby move (usually about 18–20 weeks). This is simply because the woman has probably already had an ultrasound scan and this gives us a more accurate confirmation (or otherwise) of the 'dates' and the fact that the babe is alive and kicking!

At *20 weeks* the pregnancy is half-way through. The

woman certainly looks pregnant and the baby is very definitely making its presence felt. It measures about 8 inches (from head to buttocks) and weighs an approximate 8 ounces. There is a relatively large amount of amniotic fluid, so it is able to turn complete somersaults! During these weeks of development the unborn child continues to grow and build on the foundations already laid. The very first hair appeared soon after 12 weeks; this is now replaced by a special downy hair which grows all over the body, called 'lanugo'. It is seen in very premature babies at birth. The lanugo helps a white, waxy material, 'vernix caseosa', to cling to the body. Vernix is secreted by the sebaceous glands in the skin and its function is protective. (Many babies at birth, particularly if they are a week or two early, are partly covered with vernix.) Lanugo hair is shed during the seventh month, by which time the hair on the head is well established. Incidentally, the pattern of whorls of hair is just as individual as the fingerprints.

As we approach *28 weeks* the question of 'viability' arises – the ability of the baby to live outside the womb. This is further discussed with legal considerations. However, we know that modern neonatal care has enabled many children to survive at a gestational age of less than 28 weeks. Tiny infants weighing in at a pound or so, and doing well, regularly feature in newspaper articles – we have grown to expect it!

Thankfully most babies do not arrive this early. It is not exactly known why any woman goes into labour. Certain hormones 'prime' the uterus, which then starts contracting regularly. The baby is not just the passive passenger in all this either. He or she is probably involved in the initiation of labour and also its progress. The majority of pregnancies last *40 weeks* (give or take up to 2 weeks). In these last couple of months the unborn child continues to grow and gain weight. A layer of fat covers the muscles and bones. The limbs still exercise – though, as every mother will say, the nature of the movements changes as the baby has less room in which to move around. Babies in the womb make breathing movements too – they practise their chest muscles, although the lungs are airless. Fluid fills the bronchial tubes; this is eventually squeezed out during the journey through the birth canal. The infant is then ready for his or her first gasp. Hiccoughs are also quite common *in utero* and are often felt by the mother. A pattern of wakefulness and sleep, established in the womb, may well persist into the early days of life after birth.

The special senses develop further in the few weeks prior to delivery. Even during the middle months the unborn child can tell the difference between dark and light. By birth he focuses on objects within a foot or so of the end of his nose – just the range he had *in utero*. Babies within mere hours of birth will follow objects, particularly if that 'object' is a human face.

Hearing is perhaps even better developed than sight. While in the womb the child learns the sound of his mother's voice – and the rest of the family. The background noises which fill our homes, such as radio and TV, washing machine and vacuum cleaner, filter through to the baby. The sounds are somewhat distorted (underwater) and are masked by the louder internal noises of the mother: rumblings from the intestines, her heartbeat and, loudest of all, the regular swooshing of the placenta. Advantage has been made of babies' memory of this period of their lives. Restless children have been soothed by playing recordings of 'womb music' (a mixture of loud heartbeat plus various gurgles!). It is interesting to note that all of us, whether we are right- or left-handed, tend to hold a baby with the head to our left – near the heart.

It seems that the child's emotional development starts *in utero* too. In his book *The Secret Life of the Unborn Child*, Dr Thomas Verny[4] explores this whole realm. He gathers scientific data from the world over and comes to some exciting (though at times apparently far-fetched) conclusions. He argues the case for the existence of a close level of communication between a woman and her fetus. Some of the 'old wives' tales' may turn out to have some truth in them after all. Shocks and stresses during pregnancy may indeed be transmitted to the child. He may sense the joy and happiness of being much wanted, or he senses rejection when he is not – even if the mother puts on a convincing face to the outside world that all is well. Learning patterns may be formed in the womb. Dr Verny cites examples of adults in later life instinctively knowing a piece of music, or even a foreign language(!), where the only exposure the individual had was *in utero*. Individual personalities – and hang-ups – are therefore in the making well before our arrival into this world.

As Christians we should not be surprised at all this. We have traced, in this chapter, current scientific knowledge concerning the development of the unborn child and come to the obvious conclusion that it is a continuous process. The end-point is blurred, birth being but one event along the road which leads to another clearly defined point – death. The starting-point is clearly defined – conception.

7 Defending abortion

There is a way that seems right to a man
but in the end it leads to death

Proverbs 16:25.

There are, of course, Christians who disagree with the case
which we have been making. They would generally share a
profound unease at the widespread availability of abortion
in Britain. They would agree that most, at least, of the
'social' abortions ought not to be done; the 1967 Act has
made possible something which is not far short of 'abortion
on demand'. On the other hand, they would not accept that
every abortion, unless it is done to save the mother's life, is
wrong. Sometimes, out of compassion for the mother or for
the future of the child, abortion may be right. How is this
view, held in good conscience by some Christians, defen-
ded? How is it, that is to say, that in the face of the kind of
evidence which we have discussed in the preceding chapters, such a conclusion may be reached?

BRAVE NEW PEOPLE

The fullest recent defence of this position is found in the
latest book by Professor D. Gareth Jones, *Brave New People*.[1]
This book, which addresses many of the major ethical
dilemmas confronting Christians today in the field of medical science, has itself caused considerable controversy.
Because of its defence of abortion in some circumstances
the first American edition was withdrawn by its US publisher, in the face of a major public outcry. In fact it presents
a considered and reasoned defence of abortion under very
limited conditions. We shall devote the first part of this
chapter to an examination of Professor Jones's position, as
outlined in his chapter 'The ethics of therapeutic abortion'.
It should be noted that Professor Jones's own conclusions

are apparently more conservative than those of some other Christians.

'Fetuses are human beings', Professor Jones writes, and such, as we have pointed out, may scarcely be denied; 'they are genetically part of the species, *Homo sapiens*.' But, he goes on, 'is a fetus at a particular stage of development a *person*, in the sense that it has as strong a claim to life as a normal adult human being?' He sees this as the crucial question, since 'if it is a person in this sense, it also has the claim not to be killed'.[2]

Professor Jones begins by rejecting the notion that there is a particular point in fetal development at which a line may be drawn, before which it is 'a non-person' and after which it is 'fully personal'. A variety of possible stages has been canvassed, all the way from conception to birth and, indeed, a year or so later. This suggestion is passed over in favour of the notion of 'potentiality' as governing our ethical response to the fetus. The 'potentiality principle' takes seriously the 'developmental continuum of which the fetus is a part'. We may remark in passing that the fundamental *dis*continuity is at the point of conception (fertilization), where the biological continuum begins. This marks out conception from all the other possible 'critical stages' listed in *Brave New People*, and is plainly accepted by its author as the point of departure for the process of growing potential which he takes as his ethical guide-line.

The 'potentiality principle', as Professor Jones defines it, has certain distinct implications. It does not *deny* the 'personhood' of the fetus, although 'it is prepared to assess fetal capabilities in terms of the extent of its biological development'. So, 'while fetal material is always genetically human, the very rudimentary stages of its development manifest few qualities of established personhood'. The discussion which follows is hampered by the failure to provide a working definition of either 'potentiality' (which is illustrated rather than defined) or 'personhood' (which is, of course, a term with a long history in philosophy and theology). Professor Jones is at pains to point out that such an emphasis on fetal *potential* does not imply anything other than the deepest respect for fetal life at every stage, and that the possibility of the deliberate destruction of that life can only be exceptional:

'the fetus will be protected under all normal circumstances'.

The real problem with this argument is that its terms are so loose that they can be given almost any meaning. We have already hinted at this in saying that many of those who would accept the ethical analysis set out in *Brave New People* would wish to draw wider, perhaps much wider, conclusions as to the acceptability of abortion. This is not a mere quibble about the terminology or the way in which Professor Jones sets out his case; it is rather a deep-seated difficulty with every attempt to argue for a middle position, in which the life of the fetus is given respect and yet in certain circumstances can be forfeited. In the terms of Professor Jones's own statement which is quoted at the end of our last paragraph, what is it that defines where 'normal circumstances' end and 'abnormal circumstances' begin? The fact that the author of *Brave New People* would seem to limit the 'abnormal circumstances' to certain cases of genetic disorder, while other Christian writers (such as R. F. R. Gardner, to whom we shall turn below) allow of the 'abnormality' of many other circumstances, demonstrates the essentially arbitrary nature of this kind of argumentation.

That is to say, the notion of the fetus as *potentially* a person is of little ethical help to us in weighing the claims of fetal life against other claims. We are not here arguing that the fetus *is* a person, since an answer to that question depends to such an extent on what 'person' is understood to mean.[3] The question is, what is it that the fetus is not already which it will (at birth, or viability, or whenever) later become? And what significance does this have for our attitude towards the life of the fetus and its claims upon us? *Brave New People* gives evidence of the kind of thinking behind its author's position when it says, after speaking of the degree of protection which should be accorded the fetus, that the idea of 'potentiality' is 'prepared to assess fetal capabilities in terms of the extent of its biological development'. In plain terms, what the fetus is capable of *doing* determines the extent to which its life shall be protected.

The fundamental difficulty with every criterion which depends upon *capabilities* as defining the extent of personhood (or 'potential' personhood) is that it must face the fact that the capacities which the fetus acquires (for movement, for reasoning, for relationships, and so on) are things which it can lose in later life. We do not as a rule deny that children or adults are 'persons' because they are unable to move, or to think reasonably, or to relate to others. The biblical attitude towards handicap (mental as well as physical) is one of compassion and care which implicitly recognizes the full personhood of those who suffer disability. Rather than viewing physical and mental ability as the criteria for the degree of protection which a life deserves, the dice are loaded the other way: the degree of *disability*, the weakness, unattractiveness and lack of the general attributes of human persons are what call for the special protection and concern of the people of God. The degree of fetal 'capability' is a hazardous criterion of the degree of protection which fetal life deserves.

This raises the question of the nature of human 'personhood', on which a brief comment may be made. It is very difficult to find any general definition of what a 'person' is, since we acknowledge and accept as persons human beings with a very wide range of characteristics, from babes in arms (whose abilities in any formal sense are strictly limited) to reasoning adult men and women who live in a web of sophisticated relationships, all the way to the severely subnormal and the physically handicapped – and the demented old people who make up a growing portion of our population. Any attempted definition of what it means to be a human person will fall down by failing to take account of people whose humanity and whose personhood we would not wish to deny. In so far as it adds anything to the fact that someone is a human being (a member of the species *Homo sapiens*) to say that he or she is a 'person', it makes more sense to see this as a way of recognizing that *Homo sapiens* is not merely one species among many, but is that one brought into being by God to bear his image (see chapter 1).

So *Brave New People*, in admitting that from the moment of conception the fetus is a human being, answers its own question. The suggestion that being a 'person' is something extra to being a 'human being' (and this extra thing is needed if the human being is to have 'as strong a claim to life as a normal adult human being') is unnecessary. We can leave aside the idea of 'personhood' and what it means. It is human beings who are made in the image of God, and anything which is a human being is one of us, and nothing less. The idea that something extra is required, on top of being human, to justify 'as strong a claim on life as a normal adult human being' is fraught with danger, for it rests upon the acceptance of the principle that *merely* being human does not in itself guarantee the normal regard which we have for our fellow-humans. The prospect that human beings might be designated 'non-persons' and granted less than human rights is a fearful one. Yet it is implicit even in the very limited defence of abortion which we find in *Brave New People*, and it is the same principle upon which many of the world's most barbarous regimes have operated.

We can add a comment on the idea of 'potentiality' of which this book makes so much. It is a word which covers two quite different ideas, and its usefulness in defence of abortion largely depends upon their remaining confused. In one sense something can be spoken of as 'potentially' *something else*. So a piece of waste-ground is 'potentially' a developed site, with gardens and buildings; a separate sperm and ovum are 'potentially' an embryo. But with such an idea of 'potential' there remains a fundamental distinction between what we now have (the waste-ground; the sperm and the ovum) and what we may later have (the landscaped buildings; the embryo). If we do not interfere, if we leave things as they are, nothing is going to change, and what is 'potential' will never be 'realized', but remain one of many possibilities. In another sense, however, potential can be, as we say, *built-in*. Nothing needs to be altered. What is 'potentially' present is also *already* present. And it is plainly in this sense that we can speak of the embryo and the fetus as 'potentially' human persons. So Professor T. F. Torrance writes: 'If then we want to think of the human embryo as "potentially person", that must be taken to mean, not that the embryo is in the process of becoming something else, but rather that the embryo continues to become what he or she already is.'[4] If – as is plainly the case – the fetus already is a human being, the process of becoming what we more readily recognize as a human being (and feel happier about calling a human 'person') is one of the unfolding and development of what is already present, in the first stages of the biological continuum which stretches all the way from conception to full adult maturity. Nothing is or requires to be added to the genetically complete human embryo. Like every other biological organism, including the mature human adult, the embryo's life and growth depend upon a supply of nutrients and a favourable environment. The process of realizing what is potential in the embryo, in biological and personal terms alike, does not carry any implications for the nature of the unborn human life itself. It is already what it shall be.[5]

ABORTION: THE PERSONAL DILEMMA

The publication in 1972 of R. F. R. Gardner's lengthy volume with this title was of importance in helping develop a Christian mind on the question of abortion in the United Kingdom. The scope of the volume, encompassing 'medical, social and spiritual issues', in the words of the sub-title, has made it a major resource for Christians seeking their own understanding of the question. Its 31 chapters are documented in detail, and it is no surprise that it remains in print today. Its author, who is an ordained minister as well as a Consultant Gynaecologist, is well known for his Christian commitment. Since his defence of abortion as a Christian option under certain circumstances has proved so influential, we turn to examine the way in which that defence is developed.

The essence of Mr Gardner's theological and ethical argument is spread over a series of chapters in the second part of his book under the heading, 'The Ethical Question: is abortion ever justified?' Essentially he argues for three positions. First, the fetus does not possess a soul, and therefore in this debate we are not considering the destruction of a human life destined for eternity. He suggests that it is when the child takes his or her first breath that the soul enters the body.[6] It may be objected that to speak in these terms is to employ the categories of an unbiblical anthropology, since the idea of a living human body that is soulless is unknown to Scripture. Indeed, as a writer whom Mr Gardner cites says, the soul is 'not an entity with a separate nature from the flesh. . . . Rather it is the life animating the flesh. . . . Man does not have a soul, he is a soul'.[7]

This is certainly the testimony of Genesis, where we read

that man *'became* a living being (soul)' (Genesis 2:7), not that he was entered by one. Much of the discussion of abortion among Christians takes the form of the question 'When does the soul enter the body?', but this is founded upon an unbiblical notion of the nature of man.

Three 'scientific pointers' are offered, bearing on the question of the 'spiritual status' of the fetus. First, the question of identical twins. At some point after conception, and sometimes even after implantation, the embryo divides into two. 'Unless', writes Mr Gardner, 'we are to agree with the suggestion that the soul splits likewise we are driven to conclude that in some cases at least its infusion is not before the fourth week of intrauterine life.'[8] This conclusion of course depends heavily upon the soul theory lying behind it, with the soul perceived to be a quasi-physical entity which is added to the physical human being to make him a spiritual being. In any event, part of the difficulty is removed when it is remembered that there is a hereditary element in identical twinning, which suggests that it may be genetically programmed and therefore that both twins are present in the genetic material from its first organization at fertilization onwards. If there are other cases, where by reason of external accident or other circumstance the embryo splits into two, there is still no fundamental difficulty. Plainly, where there was once one human being there are now two. Why need this imply anything about the spiritual standing of the two or of the one?

Secondly, Mr Gardner, in common with others, draws attention to the phenomenon of fetal 'wastage', whereby 'anything up to half of all conceptions end in spontaneous miscarriage, usually very early on'.[9] He considers it inconceivable that God should fill his heaven with these young lives, and concludes that it is evidence for the absence of 'spiritual status' on the part of the fetus. It is, of course, nothing of the sort, any more than the fact of very high infant mortality rates in some parts of the world is evidence for the lack of 'spiritual status' of small children. We may find it hard to understand the purposes of God in this as in other matters, but fetal wastage is not an evidence for the sub-spiritual nature of the unborn child. We discuss this further in chapter 8.

We can add here that fetal wastage had been widely used

by those who favour abortion for another purpose: to suggest that abortion is permissible because it is a human imitation of nature. In particular, the fact that many spontaneous abortions are the result of fetal abnormality leads some to argue that fetal abnormality is a proper ground for therapeutic abortion. This is a dangerous argument, since it is logically identical to an argument from the fact of high infant mortality in the Third World to the propriety of infanticide. The fact that something occurs in nature by no means implies its ethical acceptability. In fact, the practice of medicine is largely concerned with an uphill struggle *against* the suffering and death which occur 'naturally', since they are considered to be destructive and evil. In more general terms, it is of course the case that human 'wastage' is as high as 100 per cent, since man is mortal. The particular point at which mortality takes its toll – whether before implantation, *in utero*, in infancy or after three score years and ten – is but a secondary feature of the common destiny of man. The fact that every man and every woman who is conceived will at some stage die is of no special ethical relevance, any more than it is relevant to our perception of the 'spiritual status' (Gardner's phrase) of man at any other point in his brief life. Man is spiritual, but man is also mortal.

Thirdly, Mr Gardner writes of *in vitro* fertilization, referring to one of the early experiments in an area which has advanced rapidly since his volume was published in 1972. The fact that an embryo can now be cultured in a glass dish in itself tells against the 'possession of a soul' by the fetus. He asks, rhetorically, 'When the experiment is over and the material is tipped down the sluice, is a soul being destroyed?'[10] The suggestion that a 'soul' *is* present would, we read, trivialize 'the meaning of the soul'.

Having advanced these arguments and, to his satisfaction, disposed of the equation of human life with 'spiritual status', Mr Gardner turns to his own grounds for abortion. His starting-point is Christian compassion, and it is plain that it is his anxiety to be compassionate towards his patients which determines his acceptance of the practice of abortion. The Christian physician confronts the suffering of the patient and, in some cases, will feel obliged to agree to terminate the patient's pregnancy as the only adequate compassionate response. 'Real compassion', we read, 'involves taking into account the factors to be discussed in part three of this book' (medical and social questions), 'in order that one's decision will help not only the woman's short term problems, but her future life.'[11] In other words, having concluded that *prima facie* we do not need to regard the fetus as possessing the 'spiritual status' of a human being who has been born, it becomes necessary for the compassionate Christian to look at each case as it presents itself and to decide what is best for the woman. Mr Gardner does not leave altogether out of account the other party to the problem: 'We must not forget that there is to be compassion too for the fetus', he writes; but this matter is not pursued.

If abortion is an option, and compassion is the motivation, how is the Christian to· decide in individual circumstances? The third part of *Abortion: the Personal Dilemma* addresses medical and social factors which bear on the debate (with chapters, for example, on 'Illegitimate Pregnancy' and 'The Pregnant Student'). But, at the end of the day, the Christian physician's decision will be determined by his perception of the will of God: 'Before he can decide what, in this particular instance, is the compassionate decision, he must weigh up all the factors.' And there is seeming approval of the statement of an American gynaecologist: 'When a pregnancy threatens the well-being of a patient and her family I will explore the threat just as thoroughly as I would a fever, a fibroid uterus, or an ovarian cyst. Then it becomes a matter of seeking the Lord's will in each particular case. I am confident that He can guide me in these decisions as He does in other areas of life.'[12]

The importance of compassion and the perception of the will of God are not, of course, *arguments* in favour of abortion. They are rather indications of how someone who is convinced that abortion is ethically permissible goes about the practice of his principles. That is to say, we do not (at least, we should not!) come to conclusions about what is right on the basis of its being compassionate or of our feeling that we ought to do it, *unless it is already clear to us* that this thing is right in itself. It is because Mr Gardner thinks abortion to be sometimes 'right' that his compassion and his sense of the will of God are called into play. By the same token, if we are convinced that abortion is not 'right', it can hardly be said that we are lacking in compassion or in perception of the divine will if we then refuse to agree to it.

What must always be central to the Christian's thinking is the teaching of Scripture and its revelation of the will of God. Our compassion and our sense of what God wants us to do have to be informed by Scripture. The alternative is some kind of 'situation ethics', in which even the ethical guide-lines in the Bible (like 'Thou shalt not commit adultery') can be set aside out of compassion or because someone thinks that this is what the Lord wants them to do. Every attempt to make ethical decisions that does not base itself squarely on Scripture is destined to lead us astray.

OTHER RECENT DISCUSSION

Brief reference may be made to a number of recent contributions. Professor Gordon Stirrat, in *Legalised Abortion – the Continuing Dilemma*,[13] offers a distinctive understanding of the problem with which abortion confronts the Christian. For him, abortion is always wrong, and two logical and consistent alternatives present themselves – one permitting abortion only where the death of the fetus is in any case inevitable, and the other openly utilitarian, where 'the mother does have a say as to whether or not her pregnancy shall continue'.[14] The difficulty for him as for others is that, if patients and society at large do not share such a conviction, the physician is in no position to impose it. He has to live with patients who wish to avail themselves of the opportunity to have their pregnancies terminated, and he must be seen to care for them and to support them.

The problem with this kind of approach to abortion is that it fails to grasp the nature of the ethical issue that is at stake. It is plainly true as a general rule that the Christian has no right, and indeed little opportunity, to insist that those with whom he disagrees nevertheless live their lives according to his code of conduct. He would also be wrong to make their misconduct a reason for his failing to help and support them when things go wrong. But this is not the same as aiding and abetting them in doing what he knows to be wrong *when there is a third party involved*. This is the fundamental reason why those who accept that abortion involves the taking of a human life can never assent to participate in the abortion procedure (and, by statute, their participation cannot be required). For if a woman has her heart set on an abortion she is contemplating something which is not just wrong for her, but which commits the ultimate crime against her innocent child. No Christian needs to be reminded of his responsibilities towards the weak and defenceless, responsibilities which always override the freedom of others to act as they choose.

So, for example, a physician or a social worker may have laboured long to gain the confidence of a woman in distressing and difficult circumstances. But, if it emerges that she is abusing her child, the counsellor's duty to the child will always be paramount, if necessary to the extent of undermining the relationship which has been built up with the mother. He can never, in Professor Stirrat's phrase, say to her '*whatever* your decision I will support you in it and carry you through with it', because higher obligations arise from his duty to the child.

In this connection we should note an analogy drawn by Professor Oliver O'Donovan in his booklet *The Christian and the Unborn Child*.[15] The test, he writes, of an abortion policy is 'whether we are prepared to apply it in other cases' where conflicts of interest arise.

> Let us imagine a daughter caring for a difficult, but not senile, mother, in an area where neither Social Services nor neighbours were available to help her bear the load. The doctor judges that the daughter is heading for a major, and permanent, breakdown, and sees no way of avoiding it short of killing the mother. If we valued mental health equivalently to human life we might feel able to advise him to take that drastic step (provided he could get away with it). This is a conclusion from which most of us would shrink. In the last resort it is hard to accept that mental health or physical health or any *social* good is a value quite equivalent to human life. . . .[16]

R. F. R. Gardner has himself written as follows:

> Here is a woman, we will suppose, who has a house full of children. One of them, imbecile or paralysed, exhausts her

strength and monopolises her affection. In addition, she has the care of an aged and cantankerous father-in-law. And now she is pregnant yet again. So the argument is advanced: how can she be expected to cope; the burden must be reduced. I have terminated such pregnancies, and I shall do so again no doubt. But I ask myself, and I ask you, would not the same argument be equally valid to support infanticide of the imbecile child? Would it not be even more cogent to support the euthanasia of the over-demanding father-in-law?[17]

CONCLUSION

We see then that Christian defences of abortion generally operate on the principle of denying to the fetus, at some stage or at all stages, the respect due to full human life outside the womb. Sometimes this takes the form of speculation about the moment of ensoulment; sometimes it is more concerned with the development of 'personality' defined in a way that will accord with the biological development of the fetus; sometimes again it refuses to pin down any particular moment and suggests a gradual growth into that which finally (after viability, or perhaps at birth) makes full demands upon us as 'one of us'. These various proposals all fail to do justice to the biblical testimony which so plainly convinced the first Christians to take their stand against the practice of abortion in the Graeco-Roman world.

The modern developments in genetics and embryology which have emphasized the completeness of the original constitution of the conceptus, and stressed the gradual continuity of its development *in utero*, have made it increasingly difficult for any clear line to be drawn during pregnancy before and after which different moral assessments of abortion could be made. 'Viability' has become obsolete, with 'animation' and 'quickening', as the prospect of ectogenesis, the fertilization of an ovum *in vitro* and the bringing of the resulting embryo to term in an artificial womb, has disposed of the artificial principle which suggested that the coming of the fetus to a capacity for 'independent existence' was of any significance other than merely in relation to current levels of medical technology.

It is evident that serious Christian arguments for abortion

have to depend on the notion that there is such a thing as 'human life' which is not invested with the qualities we normally associate with all human life – not made in the image of God, not of infinite value to him, not destined to a future of glory or shame, not *known* by him, irrespective of its capacity for response. Only thus is it possible to claim that this thing which we know to be, like us, *Homo sapiens*, does not demand of us the reverence and the protection due to a fellow-man because of what he or she means to God. The reader must come to his own conclusion, but ours we find to be unavoidable. The notion of something that is man and yet not man, one of us and yet not one of us, a small 'somebody' and yet 'nobody' at all, is as repugnant to the teaching of Scripture as it is to human reason. It is *man*, male and female, black and white, born and unborn, whom God has made in his own image; and this truth is sealed to us and established without challenge in the coming of Jesus Christ, conceived *in utero* by the Holy Ghost.

8 Hard questions

It is hard to accept that mental health or physical health or any *social* good is a value quite equivalent to human life.

Oliver O'Donovan, *The Christian and the Unborn Child*, p.19.

1. *If abortion really is the taking of a human life, what about the case in which the mother's life is itself in danger?*

It is fortunately now very rare for a doctor to be faced with a choice between the life of the mother and that of the baby. In the later stages of pregnancy a problem can be met by recourse to Caesarean section, and the baby can be born alive. Conditions which arise in mid-pregnancy, such as high blood pressure, are now treated with the aim of getting the mother through to a stage when the baby will be viable and, though premature, has every chance of surviving. The aim is to save both patients, if that is at all possible.

What about the woman at an earlier stage of pregnancy? One important situation is that of an ectopic pregnancy, where the embryo implants outside the womb (in the fallopian tube) and the woman is in danger of bleeding to death if the tube ruptures as the pregnancy expands. It is necessary to remove the fetus or, otherwise, both it and the mother will die. Incidentally, these cases are not regarded as abortions for statistical purposes.

It becomes more difficult when we consider less acute situations. The woman with cancer of the cervix, diagnosed early in pregnancy, will not die in the next few hours if we do nothing, but she may die in a matter of months. If she is treated correctly she is offered a reasonable chance of cure, but one side-effect (of surgery or radiotherapy) will be the loss of the baby. Of course, the later the disease is discovered, the more feasible it is to allow the pregnancy to continue for a few weeks so that the baby has a reasonable chance of survival along with the mother.

There are specific medical conditions which make pregnancy inadvisable. Conditions such as highly unstable ('brittle') diabetes, chronic kidney failure and heart diseases come into this category. Such conditions often make it hard to conceive in any case, but women who succeed in becoming pregnant are frequently very determined to go through with their pregnancies – even to the extent, sometimes, of late 'booking' at the ante-natal clinic, in case they should be persuaded to have an abortion. These conditions are generally not so much life-threatening as life-shortening.

How do we assess the Christian's duty in these circumstances? In the case of an ectopic pregnancy the answer is straightforward: to allow it to continue will bring about the deaths of both mother and child, and the removal of the fetus will save one of those lives. In the later stages of pregnancy removal of the fetus should always be delayed until it is capable of life outside the womb, if this is possible. If, on the other hand, the mother is urgently in need of treatment which will, at the same time, destroy the fetus, then it may properly be decided to seek to save her life. But she must herself participate in that decision, and some women, aware of what their choice will mean, have opted instead to refuse treatment in order to save the life of the child.

2. *But is this not inconsistent? If we permit abortion for this reason, should we not also permit it for others? Is it not the thin end of a wedge?*

Not at all. Allowing life-saving treatment to the mother which also results, directly or indirectly, in the death of the baby is simply an application to pregnancy of a moral principle we recognize elsewhere. And that must be the touchstone of our thinking here. Would an argument for abortion also serve as an argument for the death of a human being in later life?

It is not difficult to think of situations in which we are, or might be, faced with such a dilemma. It is sometimes necessary, in order to save another one life, to abandon another. For instance: a mountain rescue team searches for two lost climbers. They find one of them, injured, and have to make a difficult decision. Either they take him back to safety, which will occupy all their resources and must be done without delay (since otherwise he will die), in which case they must abandon the search for the other climber, who is believed to be nearby and also injured, but alive. Or they leave the man they have found and seek the other, who will also occupy all their attention, and bring him back before he dies. They know they cannot do both. How do they make up their mind? Perhaps they decide between the climbers on the basis of their injuries (one has a better chance of survival), or on the ground of their age (the younger man might take precedence), or because one is married with small children and the other a single man without dependants. All kinds of factors might enter in, or maybe they simply do what first strikes them: take down the man they have found and worry about the other one later (though they know he will be dead). The point is that agonizing decisions like this are not unknown to us, and a pregnancy which threatens the mother's life is simply a special case of the general principles that, first, it can be right to abandon one life in order to save another; and, secondly, there are principles that help us to decide between them, if we have a choice (and here the mother's existing responsibilities and relationships may be thought to give her priority over the child, though this is not the only way of assessing the choice).

So the case of abortion to save a mother's life is not in any sense a weakening of the position which we have taken up in this book, that the life of the child before birth is human life with the dignity and rights of all human life. On the contrary, as the example of the mountaineers shows, it is an illustration of this position. The balancing of life against life arises directly from our recognition that both mother and child are human beings. The agonizing decision that may be necessary, on exceedingly rare occasions, is a decision to save life and not to take it (any more than the mountain rescue team is choosing to take the life of the mountaineer they leave behind). It is therefore more helpful to call abortion which saves the mother's life by another name, since it is an operation which is not directed at the child but at the mother.

3. *What about the malformed baby? Is it not compassionate to prevent the birth of babies with mental and physical handicaps? Is it right for the Christian to allow such suffering to be brought into the world?*

We must remind ourselves, in the emotional turmoil that surrounds these cases, that life begins at conception. Every human life is precious to God, and never before has medicine had the choice of killing the patient as a remedy for disease; and it is this which antenatal screening (discussed elsewhere in chapter 4) is encouraging us to do.

Difficulties arise when the condition diagnosed is so severe that the death of the baby is inevitable. Should the poor mother be expected to carry a doomed pregnancy for another few months, knowing that there is nothing at the end? Surely, it could be argued, the humane action would be to terminate this sort of pregnancy. Well, maybe, but there are examples of cases such as the woman who adamantly refused abortion in spite of full knowledge, on the part of the mother, that she was carrying an anencephalic. She could not countenance another abortion, having been plagued with guilt feelings after an earlier 'social' termination. The fact remains that even when the baby is bound to die (and one can be certain of this in only a relatively small proportion of cases) abortion is nevertheless the killing of a baby who is undoubtedly alive at the moment of operation, and whose only experience of life will be during his or her months in the womb of the mother.

Once the door is opened to abortion for the potentially lethal condition, decision then has to be made on behalf of the woman whose child does not have a defect which will inevitably cause death, but one which will rather result in severe handicap should he survive. Where do we draw the line? Remember that these choices of life or death (for the baby) are made fairly early in pregnancy. No diagnostic tool is failproof. What happens in practice is that the conditions that are diagnosable are 'treated' with abortion, while those which are not escape notice until birth. In other words, if the alphafetoprotein is raised indicating an 'open' spina bifida, abortion would be offered (in practice often recommended) whatever the degree of defect. Down's syndrome may be diagnosed, so these children are aborted – though this abnormality is not nearly as devastating as certain other congenital problems.

Sometimes the child's condition is not itself amenable to diagnosis and decisions are based on probability statistics. For example, if a woman contracts rubella (German measles) during the first three months of pregnancy there is a 50 per cent risk that the fetus may have developed an abnormality (of heart, ear, eye, brain or some combination). The only *certain* method of diagnosis, however, is to find the virus in the tissues of the aborted fetus.

With any congenital deformity or disease which is particularly severe, the baby will die in any case. Where it is not, the baby will live, and if the parents and/or doctors wish otherwise, then they must take active steps to ensure its demise.

The Christian assessment of this ground for abortion must begin by recognizing what it is that we are talking about. People often speak of it as the *prevention* of handicap, or as some kind of *cure* for the conditions which can be diagnosed during pregnancy. But this is not true. The child is already handicapped (that is why the condition can be diagnosed), and he or she is 'cured' by being killed. Of course, the parents are saved great distress, and the welfare state great expense, in cases of severe abnormality. But Christians have never before believed it to be right to show compassion towards the diseased by destroying them.

In fact, the Bible is much concerned with questions of disability and handicap, and Jesus' ministry to the blind and the lame revealed a special concern for them on the part of God which has been passed on to the people of God. The Scriptures look forward to a time when 'the lame will leap like a deer, and the tongue of the dumb shout for joy' (Isaiah 35:5–6). To propose the destruction of the handicapped (whether after birth or before) is seriously to deny the meaning which the Bible gives to compassion.

4. *What of the case in which pregnancy comes about as a result of rape, or incest, or in the very young? Are these distressing situations not exceptions to the rule?*

Rape is always emotive. When the Abortion Bill was formulated in the 1960s a clause dealing with rape as an indication for legal abortion was included. This was dropped because of the difficulties of defining and proving it. One of the interesting facts surrounding the *Rex v. Bourne* case is that, while rape was one of the grounds on which Mr Bourne felt that termination of pregnancy was indicated, no prosecution was ever brought to bear on the soldier who presumably committed the guilty act.

It should also be noted that pregnancy arising from rape is unusual.

Does it present a real exception to the rule? The fact that rape is such a dreadful crime should not blunt our awareness of the fact that the child conceived by rape is a wholly innocent party. We need also to note that the child is likely to be healthy and the pregnancy without any special problems. It is a matter of judgment in individual cases whether the trauma of an abortion or the continuation of the pregnancy (followed perhaps by the adoption of the child) is likely in the long term to have significant effects on the woman in addition to those of the rape itself. Although she is filled with revulsion by what has happened, the woman needs to be reminded that the child she is carrying is her own child as well as that of the father. To destroy this (innocent) third party will merely add to the evil which has already been done.

The same point needs to be made when we come to incest, although the problem is rather different. Pregnancy is much rarer. Often a child has been abused before she becomes fertile. If pregnancy does occur there is a more than usual risk of genetic abnormality – recessive genes may make their appearance. Whatever the worries might be concerning the pregnancy though, it is obvious that the psychological hang-ups that the unfortunate girl is bound to have run much deeper than that. The pregnancy may be the least of her problems. She will probably have emotional scars for many years to come, if not for the rest of her life, and abortion will not relieve them, may compound them, and is inflicted upon an innocent party who is also her child. It is a tragic irony that after suffering so dreadfully at the hand of her own parent she should be encouraged to do this dreadful thing to her own child.

The very young teenager may be pregnant as a result of abuse, though usually it is through a more normal relationship. As girls mature earlier physically (though not necessarily emotionally), early pregnancy becomes a commoner event. In 1980 nearly a thousand abortions in England and Wales were performed on teenagers under the age of 15. Teenage pregnancy has been studied (Professor J. K. Russell has recently published a book devoted to the subject) and shown to have on the whole a surprisingly uncomplicated course. The mother's skeleton, sometimes still growing, accommodates the baby in labour by virtue of its greater elasticity, and the joints of the pelvis give more easily than those of a mature adult. Another interesting phenomenon is the amazing ability (which applies to adults with other diseases too) to shut off what is happening in one part of the body. So, a young girl can be playing with her doll at one end, uninterested in the labour which is in progress at the other!

The second point that must be stressed is the hazard associated with abortion in the very young. The more immature the cervix, the harder it is to dilate it. The very patients who might seem to warrant abortion by virtue of their youth may be the ones whose future child-bearing capacity is most put at risk by the operation. The damaged cervix may become 'incompetent', causing recurrent miscarriage in subsequent pregnancies. It should be added that a special problem with teenage pregnancy (together with pregnancy in the mentally subnormal) is that it is often concealed, deliberately or because unrecognized, until it is more than half-way completed and too late for an abortion in any case.

What needs to be borne in mind in all these cases (and they are surely the most serious of all 'social' arguments for abortion, although the social circumstances of other pregnant women can present distressing problems) is that none of these cases presents an argument for destroying a human life. If the fetus were anything less than a miniature human being, then these cases might offer grounds for its destruction. But since it is not a lump of jelly but one of us, created in the image of God and destined for eternity, these cases argue for its destruction no more strongly than they would for the destruction of the life of a child already born.

5. *But even if we grant that the position which you are arguing is the Christian position, what right have I (as a doctor, a nurse, a social worker, or just a citizen) to impose my convictions on others who see things differently?*

The first thing to note is that there is a real difference between giving people the liberty to make their own decisions (for good or ill) and, on the other hand, *collaborating* with them and assisting them in carrying out what we believe to be wrong courses of action. Whether as someone professionally involved or simply as a friend, if I contribute in some way to the decision to carry out an abortion (or to the act itself), then I am not just refraining from imposing my own views, I am helping do something I know to be wrong.

But this would equally be true of other acts (like, let us say, working for a publisher of pornographic books). In the case of abortion something else arises: there is a third party involved, another human being to consider – the child. We have, as Christians, responsibilities to our neighbours, and as Jesus made clear, *every* human being is our neighbour. Our obligations to the child outweigh any conceivable duty we may owe to the mother to respect her choice in the matter. This does not mean that the Christian who takes this view will find it easy to decide what he will and will not do, if he is in any way involved with abortion in a practical way. There are doctors who will not see women who are seeking abortion advice; there are others who will see them and discuss the matter even though they will always come to the same conclusion – and perhaps pass some patients on to a colleague who might take a different view. There is a great range of practical options. But it is hard to see how someone who believes the unborn child to be a human being could ever consent to sign the green form which authorizes the operation.

Nurses also have very special problems, as we have already mentioned (see chapter 5). Some refuse to have anything to do with abortion, to the extent of declining to be involved in the after-care of those who have had the operation. Others limit their conscientious objection to participation in the operation itself and its preparations.

If abortion is in fact the destruction of a human life, the

conscientious Christian, at whatever cost to his or her career and sometimes with considerable difficulty, will wish to distance himself or herself from this dreadful act.

6. *Does not the recognition of conception as the point at which human life begins imply that some methods of 'contraception' widely in use today – which work by preventing the embryo from implanting in the womb – must be wrong?*

The answer to this question is certainly 'Yes'. As we have shown elsewhere (see chapter 4) the intra-uterine 'contraceptive' device (IUCD) and certain other methods are in fact not *contraceptives* at all, but *abortives*. That is to say, they do not prevent the fertilization of the ovum, but instead prevent the already fertilized ovum (in the first days of pregnancy) from implanting in the womb, and thus produce an early abortion. Women who regularly use such methods will, if they are fertile, have repeated abortions (without being aware of the fact).

7. *Must it not be the case, then, if spontaneous and induced abortion from the very start of pregnancy in fact have the effect of destroying tiny human beings, that there will be great numbers of immature humans in heaven?*

Plainly this follows, but to suggest that this is in some way an objection to the idea of conception as the beginning of human life is to overlook a number of factors. Most important is that, with one proviso, the fact of infant mortality (which is and always has been at very high rates in under-developed societies) will ensure that this is so in any case. The proviso is that we assume that those dying in infancy are in fact destined to go to heaven, which is of course another question. The case in favour of infants going to glory does not need to depend upon liberal notions of the sinlessness of childhood, with which conservative Christians would not hold. On the contrary, the same result can be seen as a fruit of election, God's sovereign choice of those whom he pleases to be with him in glory. That is to say, God might have chosen to elect to salvation all those who would in fact die in infancy.

But the important thing to note is that the problem of the

eternal destiny of those dying *in utero* is the same as that of
those dying in infancy – it simply adds to the numbers
involved. And it is no new problem. We have quoted
Augustine in this respect, and it is worth looking again at
his own assessment of the problem:

> I fail to see why, if they [the fruits of abortion] are not excluded
> from the number of the dead, they shall not attain to the resur-
> rection of the dead. . . . I do not see how. . . . even those who
> died in their mother's womb shall have no resurrection.

And he goes on to make the connection which we have just
made:

> We must at least apply to them, if they rise again, all that we
> have to say of infants who have been born.[1]

Our notions of heaven are, of course, a little blurred. We
do not know what *we* shall be doing there, so we cannot
speculate on the destiny of human lives which have never
come near to maturity. We face the related question (which,
interestingly, Augustine goes on to discuss in his next
chapter) of whether those dying in infancy will be raised in
their infants' bodies, or in the maturity to which they
would have come. Perhaps there is a hint to us in the
parables of our Lord which suggest that we (mature adult
believers?) shall be engaged in positions of responsibility.

Perhaps there is also a hint in the Bible's references to
children praising God. Psalm 8 takes up this theme,
addressing the Lord as 'Thou whose glory above the
heavens is chanted by the mouth of babes and infants'
(Psalm 8:1–2a, RSV). Whatever we make of texts such as
these, we face the problem of infants in glory with or
without a belief in the human nature of the child *in utero*.
Granted the lack of information we have about the future
life, the objection which this question implies is akin to that
of the Sadducees, who sought to disprove the idea of
heaven by raising the problem of those who had been
married more than once. Our Lord made short work of the
problem.

POSTSCRIPT: PASTORAL QUESTIONS

This book, like most books, consists mainly of arguments. But abortion, and the issues which revolve around it, involve people in the most personal and sometimes the most dreadful of all their decisions. We know that very well, and we know also that for every ten or twenty people who read this book there will be one or two for whom it touches on deep and personal things. Some of them – some of you for whom we write – have had an abortion, maybe more than one; possibly long ago, perhaps even in secret from your friends. Some may even now be considering whether they *ought* to have one, carrying a child whom for one reason or another they do not want to bring to birth. Others will have miscarried during a past pregnancy, and may find disturbing memories aroused as they think of the fate of the unborn.

So we have written this short postscript. It is hardly a substitute for the kind of care and counsel which some of those who read this book will need. But it is a brief opportunity for us to acknowledge the uneasy and sometimes even anguished feelings which can come to the surface when women consider their unborn children.

We have written three statements below: one to those who have miscarried, one to those who are pregnant and do not want to be, and one to those readers who have already had an abortion.

Miscarriage
The term 'miscarriage' is usually used these days for what strictly speaking should be called a 'spontaneous abortion'. This is clearly to distinguish this upsetting event from an induced abortion, often simply called an 'abortion'.

Miscarriage is a common event, roughly estimated as occurring at least once in every fifth pregnancy. Studies performed on women having regular, unprotected intercourse suggest that when the sensitive hormone tests to detect very early (days old) pregnancy are applied, a considerably greater proportion of loss is revealed.

The vast majority of women having a miscarriage will go on to a successful pregnancy 'next time'. A few unfortunate ones may have some abnormality of the womb, or a major inherited problem in the embryo which makes miscarriage a repeated event – 'habitual abortion', as it is sometimes called. Tests can often elucidate the nature of such problems.

It is a fact – and this is being increasingly realized – that women losing a pregnancy, even at an early stage, need to grieve and work through their feelings in similar fashion to the mother losing a baby through stillbirth, or even later, after birth. Whereas in years past the products of a spontaneous abortion were whisked away by the medical attendants, it is now appreciated that some women need to see the fetus. In the same way mothers are now encouraged to see their stillborn babies – sometimes photographs are taken – as this helps them to come to terms with what has happened and enables a more natural grief reaction.

When miscarriage occurs as early as 6 to 8 weeks' gestation it may well be 'complete', but at later stages it is usual to perform curettage of the uterus to ensure complete emptying of the womb. The experiences of women in hospital vary tremendously according to the education and motivation of nurses and doctors, but we hope there will be improvement with a better understanding of the emotional needs of women in this situation. For like every experience of bereavement, miscarriage can be lonely. There is no-one else who quite understands what you are going through. It is difficult even for your husband to be sympathetic in the way you might like, because he is often concerned for you more than for the baby you have lost. There is still a tendency for doctors and others to play down what has happened, but playing down a death is never a real help. How much you will grieve for the baby will depend on many things (you become more attached to the baby as the pregnancy progresses, so an early miscarriage may be far less traumatic than a stillbirth; but we are all different, and for some it can be an experience which it will take many months to get over).

Much of the unease about miscarriage stems from confusion as to what has happened. Is it a baby who has died, or merely something less than that? We have shown in the preceding pages that the product of conception is indeed an unborn baby, so if he or she dies from natural causes (just as if he or she dies in an induced abortion), then *a baby has died*. Recognizing that may be the first step to coming to terms with miscarriage.

This does not mean that it is ever right, or healthy, to become preoccupied with what has happened. But a period of grieving is often necessary when we face death near at hand, and for many women this will be the way to cope with their sadness. If there are no medical difficulties, another pregnancy a few months later provides the antidote to an over-preoccupation with miscarriage.

A useful book which gives a full treatment of the subject is *Miscarriage* by Ann Oakley, Ann McPherson and Helen Roberts (Collins Fontana, 1984).

Unwanted pregnancy

This term covers many different attitudes towards pregnancy, and it is probably unfair to some of those who are considering abortion to use it of them, lumping them together with women for whom their pregnancy is merely an inconvenience. Christians are unlikely to find themselves in this latter category. If a Christian woman is considering an abortion, it is probably for a very serious reason.

We have looked at many of these reasons in the course of the book. The possibility of fetal handicap (perhaps particularly after the mother has contracted German measles) is a reason why many women come under pressure from doctors and others to end their pregnancies, and a reason which carries weight with some Christians. Others may simply feel they cannot cope with another child, and many a woman has been asked by her doctor, when her pregnancy test has been confirmed, whether she wants to proceed with the pregnancy – if he thinks the conception was unplanned. This immediately raises difficulties in many women's minds, since – on one level – there are often all kinds of reasons why it would be better if she were not pregnant. The family might have come to depend financially on her job, or she might already feel overstretched with two or three small children, or her husband (who may see things differently – he may not take her own moral view) may have expressed himself strongly against their having more children.

It is well known that pregnancy produces many changes

in the mother's body, some of which result in her being emotionally sensitive. She is not in the best frame of mind to make any important decision, let alone a decision of this magnitude. And, despite the wording and intentions of the 1967 Abortion Act, it is largely up to the pregnant mother to decide whether she wants to abort her baby. If she is under pressure to do so, she may find it difficult to resist.

There is nothing more important to remember than the goodness and providence of God. The Christian who finds herself in this situation will want to pray and to seek him, setting her problem before him. Like so many of our problems, it may seem to be insoluble. But put before God, alongside the fact that in his providence he has brought into being another human life in the womb of the mother, the problem will be seen in perspective.

There are many other things the mother can do. She can seek the help of her minister, she can contact one of the counselling agencies who exist to help people like her, she can confide in sympathetic friends. What she must never lose sight of is that she is no longer alone. Unseen and unheard, though soon to be felt, there is another life pulsating within her body. Whether he or she will be 'normal' or with some degree of handicap, and whether or not the pregnancy was expected, the little child she already bears will soon be born and become the object of her love. If for some compelling reason (like, perhaps, the strength of feeling of her husband) the baby cannot be given a home in her family, there are many other families who would love to make the baby theirs instead. One of the tragic consequences of abortion has been to cut down the number of babies available for adoption, since liberal abortion has made possible an easier and quicker way out of the responsibilities of parenthood than carrying the child to term and then giving him or her up for adoption. Yet this course is always open in extreme cases where the mother is unable to care for her offspring.

Abortion
Since there have been more than two million abortions under the 1967 Act, there are well over one million mothers in this country whose babies' lives have been ended in this way, allowing for overseas visitors (many of whom come

here to have abortions) and those who have had more than one. For all kinds of reasons, and with various degrees of responsibility, there are many Christians who fall into this category.

Some have aborted with a heavy heart; others without thought to what they have done. Some have been advised that Protestants consider abortion to be all right. Some have had abortions in secret, out of sight of their church, or perhaps their husbands; maybe to conceal an illicit relationship. What all these and many more have in common is that they have destroyed the fruit of their womb, and it will not have left their consciences unmarked.

Christians believe in forgiveness, and forgiveness comes from God. It comes from him through Jesus Christ, and it comes in response to repentance. That is to say, we do not deal with our wrongdoings by playing them down; we deal with them by playing them up, recognizing them to be as black as they really are, and admitting them to God. It is then that we can be forgiven.

So if you have had an abortion, whether years back or in the last few months, you must go to God and tell him that you realize the awful nature of what you have done, and you must ask to be forgiven.

You should also tell someone else, perhaps your minister, and ask him to help you deal with this as with anything else that leaves the conscience ill at ease. Not that you are alone to blame – indeed, you may be much less blameworthy than those who counselled you and those who performed the operation itself. But the process of seeking forgiveness begins with a proper assessment of the apportioning of blame, and this is something which, in this case, will need an outsider's help.

But do not forget, however dark your conscience, that God will forgive. There is no sin too great, and with forgiveness comes a new beginning.

9 All our tomorrows

> We need to raise the ethical questions with a serious and not a frivolous conscience. A man of frivolous conscience announces that there are ethical quandaries ahead that we must consider before the future catches up with us. By this he often means that we need to devise a new ethic that will provide rationalization for doing in the future what men are bound to do because of new actions and interventions science will have made possible. In contrast, a man of serious conscience means to say in raising urgent ethical questions that there may be some things that men *should never do*. The good things men do can be made complete only by the things they *refuse to do*.
>
> Paul Ramsey, *Fabricated Man*, pp. 122–123.

ETHICS AND EMBRYOS

The publication in Britain in 1984 of the Warnock Report, the result of two years of deliberation by a government-appointed committee into the rapid advances in medical technology and science, has precipitated major public ethical debate of a kind unknown before. What its outcome will ultimately be cannot be foreseen. Indeed, so swift is the pace of change that we do not know even the questions which we shall face as each new year opens. The watershed marked by Warnock is of special significance for this discussion because of the relation of abortion with *in vitro* fertilization and its consequences.

For one thing, the experience of nearly two decades of a liberal abortion policy has prepared medical and public opinion for possibilities which would otherwise have been excluded. Thus the experimental use of human embryos, by means of which the IVF programme has been developed and sustained, is easily justified by physicians and presented to the public when abortion for trivial reasons has become a commonplace of their experience.[1]

At an ethical level this need not be so. The ethical justification of abortion generally takes the form of a 'conflict of rights', in which maternal rights take precedence over fetal rights. When fetal rights are given little weight, relatively trivial maternal reasons become substantial enough to justify what the mother wants. This is an altogether different scenario from that in which embryos are used for purposes of research. Here, what are pitched against the rights of the embryo are not those of a named individual who, because of her relationship with the embryo, has special rights over it, but 'society', 'science', 'research' and its great importance to us all.

Scientific research might seem a much more worthy cause in which to destroy an embryo than a mother's desire not to continue with a pregnancy. But we are in a different game. The unborn child, whose rights could be set against those of his or her mother, even though he or she might lose out (because the mother's rights carry more weight with those in a position to decide), has suddenly come to have no rights at all. *He* or *she* has become an *it*. What was, to use the term which means so little but appeals to so many, a 'potential person', has become a 'laboratory artifact', mere 'human material', to quote another phrase which is becoming popular.

So an embryo, which was once protected in law and in morality unless and until it could be shown to pose a threat to the mother's well-being (or that of her family), has become an experimental object which may not only be *destroyed*, but may be *created*, for purposes of laboratory research. In an important sense, therefore, the experimental use of the embryo takes us on to another stage, beyond abortion, away from the Christian view of man.

The problem is this. If the arguments used (by Warnock and others) to support a *limited* research programme are in fact as weak as they seem, it will be merely a matter of time before they are seen to break down and to take with them whatever legislative and other controls they may have created. For example, if an embryo up to 14 days' gestation can be used for experimental purposes and then destroyed, on the ground that at this stage it is without any kind of feeling or 'sentience', what argument is there against the use of *other* 'human material' under similar conditions for similar purposes? So, why should not the product of a late abortion be sustained artificially and, if need be, suitably anaesthetized so as not to feel pain, and then employed for experimental purposes? In fact aborted fetuses are already being used in this way (without, we should add, anaesthesia).[2]

Again, it is said by many that there is a fundamental difference in nature between an embryo fertilized *in vitro* with the express purpose of implantation, and one fertilized *in vitro* without any such purpose, the fusion of donated semen and a donated egg intended for mere research. This is a persuasive argument, and has convinced many. But it rests on the assumption that the embryo's rights derive from what people wish to do with it, not from what it is in itself, which is a strange way of seeing things. It has similarities with the way in which physicians confront a late abortion, on the one hand, and a premature delivery on the other. If the abortion is at 26 weeks they will intend the baby to die, and if need be they may leave it for five or ten minutes while it dies. The same physician and the same nurses may then struggle to sustain the life of another fetus also of 26 weeks, who may then survive. What is the difference between the two? Nothing, except the intentions of those involved – mother and medical staff.

A similar situation has arisen in cases of neo-natal care, where a new-born baby is found to be handicapped and his parents and the doctor in charge decide what is to be done. There is evidence that sometimes, and increasingly, the life of the child will depend upon such a discussion. Will steps be taken to save the child, or will occasion be found to bring about his or her death, by acts of commission or omission? The frightening spectre which must now be raised is of the application to this situation of the logic of embryo research. If the parents are agreeable (or do not care), if the baby is suitably anaesthetized so that he or she does not feel pain, might not the interests of all concerned appear well served by his use for some important experimental function? Would this not be better, we can hear it argued, than his dying fruitlessly?

And so we could go on, with each scene more disturbing than the last. What about unwanted babies, handicapped or not, who could be kept alive, suitably drugged, for years

116

of laboratory service? What about the unwanted elderly, dementing and uncaring, who might also make major contributions to scientific advance (perhaps, we can hear it plausibly said, into a better understanding of the causes of dementia)?

All of this follows, and it follows relentlessly, from the first decision that a member of our species, the fruit of human conception, 'one of us', may be used, for the benefit of the 'rest of us', as an experimental object. The criteria are the same: there is no feeling, there is no caring on the part of the subject, and no-one else is unhappy who is close to the person concerned. The kind of compelling individual arguments which can be imagined would seem irresistible at each stage in the process. For example, it is already being said that, with embryos available for research, the thalidomide tragedy would never have occurred.

We might each be invited to carry cards like Kidney Donor Cards (so as to emphasize the voluntary nature of the scheme) which specified that, in the event of our receiving injuries or falling ill in particular ways, we would not be resuscitated in the normal way, but our living bodies given for living research. The next step, of course, would be for us to be asked to carry cards if we did *not* wish to be part of the voluntary programme, since the shortage of volunteers was causing problems. It would of course be possible for certain categories of person to be committed to such a programme without volunteering at all, either because of illness or injury, or perhaps criminality, or something else. In Nazi Germany the victims of just such a programme (although without benefit of anaesthetics) were selected because they were Jews, and committed to Josef Mengele, camp physician at Auschwitz. But of course, it would be said, the voluntary and painless character of our programme would distinguish it entirely from that barbaric episode.

THE CRITERIA FOR DISPOSAL

Such a picture of the future is not difficult to draw, using the criteria which defenders of the new medicine and its ethics have already outlined. The relevance of the implications of the *in vitro* fertilization programme for our discussion is this: it is our case, outlined on scientific, biblical and general philosophical grounds in the chapters above, that abortion other than as a means of saving the mother's life depends logically upon the use of some criterion which will distinguish the life of the unborn (either until birth itself, or until some point in its gestation prior to birth) from the life of the human person who has been born. This is necessary, since otherwise (if it is admitted that there is no such criterion) the arguments used in favour of the abortion would also be usable in favour of the killing of, say, a member of the family of a patient in distress whose death might reasonably be held to alleviate the patient's mental or physical condition.

Since no-one would argue in favour of the general killing of persons for the benefit of others (except in limited cases such as severe handicap or dementing old age), then some criterion must distinguish the unborn from the born, whatever it may be. And there is no shortage of such criteria. Indeed, it is one of the most powerful arguments against any one criterion that it is simply one out of many possibles, some of which are found compelling to one group of people, others to another group.

What is the criterion to be? We have listed many in these pages. The Aristotelian notion of 'animation', taken over by the medieval church, has been one. Although the church never used it as an argument for abortion, it brought within the church the principle of such a dividing-line in the continuum of human life. 'Quickening' has had a long tradition of significance, the point in pregnancy when the mother first begins to feel the fetus moving. In English law a pregnant woman could be hanged before, but not after, quickening. In practical terms the major criterion of recent years has been that of 'viability', the point at which the fetus may survive outside the womb. The legal importance of this point stems from the provisions of the Infant Life (Preservation) Act (1929), according to which a fetus 'capable of being born alive' is protected. Advances in neo-natal technology have been so considerable that a figure of around 24 weeks is probably necessary now, and there is no practical reason why further improvements should not push the point back while developments in *in vitro* technology push forward ability to sustain fetal life until the two meet mid-way. Research on an artificial womb has long been in progress and could be crowned with success in the not-too-distant future. Every embryo and fetus would then be 'viable', and the criterion would disappear altogether.

Other criteria include, at one end, the first breath drawn by the baby, and, at the other, the development of the 'primitive streak' in the early embryo (or some other early stage in its growth). And, alongside such fixed criteria, we have notions of 'growing potential' which refuse to fix a point before which abortion is acceptable and after which it is not, but which agree that, say, before 6 weeks it is plainly all right, after 28 weeks plainly not, and in between it is hard to say because, at *some* indeterminate point between 6 and 28 weeks, the moral balance swings across.

These are all possible criteria setting out to distinguish, in some essential manner, between the subject for whom the termination of life is an option and the subject for whom it is not. Our contention is that none of these criteria is satisfactory. At no point is it possible to draw the moral line which each of these principles attempts, in defence of an act in one circumstance which is acknowledged to be indefensible in another. The steady erosion of the one which had perhaps the most appearance of objectivity and usefulness – that of viability – reveals the subjectivity of this entire attempt to make moral distinctions when confronted by a deep continuity in the life of embryo and fetus, from the creation of the genotype at fertilization right through to birth, childhood and adult maturity. It needs to be remembered that any candidate proposed for the role of such a criterion must be capable of bearing a weight which is immense. Upon it must depend not merely an abortion policy, but the entire concept of the rights of man.

This was the point being illustrated in the scenario we earlier sketched of possible developments following on from an acceptance of deleterious experimentation upon human embryos. In both of these (related) cases an artificial line has been drawn (at 14 days, or thereabouts, in the one case and 28 weeks in the other) to permit the unborn human being to be treated in a way in which it would be unthinkable to treat it at a later stage: as an experimental object, or as a sacrifice to the convenience of the mother. If the basic position of this book is correct and all such criteria are arbitrary, it is not merely likely, it is inevitable, that the treatment accorded to humans 'before' will in due course be accorded to them also 'after', since with the passage of time all arbitrary distinctions collapse as their inner logic asserts itself. That is why we need to appreciate what is really at stake in these debates. This may be illustrated by two examples.

VIABILITY AND HANDICAP

First, that of *viability*. There can be no doubt that this idea has been the practical ethical principle underlying public and medical acceptance of abortion. There would *seem* to be a difference in kind between a fetus which is incapable of 'independent life' (and may thus be considered some kind of maternal appendage) and one which can thrive outside the womb. In fact this distinction rests on ignorance, since *in utero* the fetus is already an independent life-system, depending on the mother only for a suitable environment and suitable nutrients; and the neo-nate, outside the womb, remains wholly dependent upon the mother (or others) for these very things. As the stage of gestation at which viability may be assumed has steadily moved downwards from around 30 towards 20 weeks, developments in neo-natal care have illustrated the identity of fetal 'dependence' inside and outside the womb.

The response of the practical ethics of medical bodies who advise government in these matters has been to suggest a lowering of the upper date for termination of pregnancy, which is consistent with their use of viability as the effective criterion. Yet, we must ask, what will their reaction be when, as may happen in twenty years' time, it becomes possible to reduce the age at which the fetus can survive outside the womb from something over 20 weeks to, say, something over 15; and then, at another stage, when with the development of an artificial placenta and the possibility of ectogenesis, it becomes possible to do away altogether with the idea that there is a stage at which the fetus *in utero* passes from being incapable of life outside to a 'viable' status? This is an important question.

Perhaps the answer lies in resistance to the World Health

Organisation's proposal of a lowering of the maximum age for abortion on this ground to 22 weeks, since diagnosis of fetal abnormality may not be possible by then. That is to say, the criterion of viability has come to be seen to have exceptions. Sometimes even a viable fetus should be destroyed. As neo-natal and *in vitro* technology improve, it will become true that every fetus is a viable fetus, and this attempted distinction between those human beings who can be and those who cannot be destroyed will have failed, and be seen to have failed. Its essentially arbitrary character will be plain to all.

The second, and related, example is that of *the care of new-born babies who are handicapped*. There are difficult questions here, and we are not arguing that every technological means must be employed to prolong the life of every baby, including those whose life expectancy is anyway very limited (though neither are we arguing the contrary). What is plain is that, in some hospitals, babies whose handicaps are by no means the most serious – in particular, babies born with Down's syndrome – are sometimes deliberately killed. As the recent and celebrated Arthur case, in which a paediatrician was tried for murder, made clear, some doctors make a practice, for example, of sedating babies so that they do not cry for food, or in some other fashion (direct or indirect) of bringing about their death.

What is it that these examples show? They illustrate the movement in medical ethics which is inherent in the instability produced by the present arbitrary criteria which decide where human life that is sacred ends, and human life that is disposable begins. What some are calling neo-natal euthanasia (though the simpler term is infanticide) is a reasonable step along the road from the widely accepted practice of abortion on the grounds of fetal handicap. It is seen as a way of dealing with abortion cases which have slipped through the net. Of course this is one of the more stringent grounds for abortion, and only a small minority of cases are aborted for this reason. It is also one of the grounds which appeals to many Christians, who regard it as compassionate to the mother and (in some strange fashion) to the child. But it is fundamentally inconsistent to allow abortion for fetal handicap and deny a selective neo-natal euthanasia. Indeed, in a recent letter to *The Times*, written in reply to one of the present writers who had drawn attention to the extension of abortion into neo-natal care, both the President and the Secretary of the British Paediatric Association felt it necessary to deny that this was the practice of 'the very great majority' of paediatricians, while candidly admitting the fundamental inconsistency which was involved in accepting abortion but not infanticide.[3]

How long, we may ask, will it be before the present practice of some paediatricians who bring about the deaths of handicapped babies results (perhaps as a consequence of another prosecution of a doctor for murder) in legislation for a limited policy of infanticide (where the parents, say, sign a form that they do not want the child, and in the opinion of two physicians in good faith the child cannot be expected to enjoy life of a certain quality)?

It is ironic that recent years have witnessed a growing interest in the rights and dignities of the handicapped, and yet hand in hand has come a notion of compassion which would not *prevent* handicap but destroy those (born or unborn) who are already its victims. It would be a small step from the present practice of some eminent paediatricians to the view of some leading ethicists and, indeed, famous Nobel prize-winners, that new-born babies should be given a thorough examination which they would have to pass before they could be considered fit to be citizens.[4] If they failed, they would, of course, be destroyed. It would also be only a short step to a similar approach to the problems of handicap in later life, and to the problem which old age presents. If a fetus should die because of its handicap, if a new-born baby should die for the same reason, why not an older handicapped person who would otherwise be a burden on family and state, and, it may be, a cause of distress and anguish over many years? What about those who become handicapped through serious injury – is it right that they should be saved, at great expense to the health services, 'only' to become burdens on those around them and the welfare provisions of the nation? Should not the elderly who become unable to care for themselves through incontinence or dementia, or one of the many other conditions which incapacitate old people, also be considered for disposal? The quality of their life may be very low, and the prospect of years in an institution (particularly one starved of funds) may not seem pleasant.

Already there is a wide feeling that senile dementia (the quality of 'wandering' and being out of touch with reality which afflicts many old people) is a reason for not treating relatively straightforward ailments. That is to say, people who are dementing but otherwise fit and healthy are being allowed to die by doctors who fail to treat a relatively straightforward problem. Their supposedly low 'quality of life' (though they may seem very contented in their abstracted way) and the burden of their care upon the state are considered grounds for taking advantage of the opportunity presented by some temporary problem to bring about their death. There are Christians who would take this approach, and it could easily be enshrined one day in legislation and provide an effective means of disposing of some of our elderly population by a policy of active euthanasia.

This all raises the question of the kind of society we want. Is it one in which everyone is fit and healthy, and those who are not, unless they can readily be cured, are marked for disposal? Or rather do we seek a society that shows respect to all its people, without regard for their ability or disability, and which deploys its resources as best it can to care for them all? In opting for abortion as a response to fetal handicap we seem to have chosen one path rather than the other.

WHAT KIND OF SOCIETY?

Concern for the kind of society we want is not, of course, the chief factor in the Christian's thinking. It is sometimes the case that we must do what is right and leave the consequences to God. But, in this instance, there is no such conflict. For many centuries the Bible's teaching that human life is sacred laid the foundations of civilized society and led, as its implications have been thought through, to our modern concern for the weak and the disabled and the sick. The Hippocratic tradition in medicine, with its explicit repudiation of the ancient as well as modern evil of abortion, has led to the development of medicine as a distinctly Christian calling. It is no surprise that medical missions have been foremost in planting the gospel in countries all across the world.

But this ancient tradition, uniting the best insights of the physicians of Greece with the teaching of Old and New Testaments, and reinforced by the detestation of both Jews and early Christians for the destruction of the unborn, has in our own generation come under threat. The sacred dignity of human life, given by God and for him alone to take away, is now thought by some to be at the disposal of man. The early embryo, genetically perfect and undoubtedly human, is treated with all the dignity and reverence accorded to a laboratory rat, to be sacrificed by experiment in the cause of science. The fetus, its developing body increasingly recognizable as one of us, with limbs and eyes and ears and mouth apparent from an early stage, with beating heart and pumping blood and growing brain, a boy or a girl in miniature – the fetus finds his or her life at risk. At risk because he or she is an inconvenience, small or great, to mother and to her world. Perhaps she had not intended to conceive, and is distressed at the prospect of a baby in her care – a first one (she may not be married) or one too many (there may be real problems in the family already born). Perhaps this child himself, or herself, is not all that he or she was hoped to be. In body or in mind there is, the doctor tells the mother, something wrong. Perhaps . . . there are today many 'perhapses' in the weeks and months of early life for the new baby, all unknowing, in the mother's womb – perhaps for some other cause this little life is under threat and will be ended by the surgeon's instruments before it sees its mother's face. Perhaps, slipping through the net, the child is born with some deformity. The parents do not want to know, the doctor feels he has the right, and by some means or other the handicapped new-born will never grow up to join those other handicapped whose rights are rightly trumpeted in a society which cares.

The Christian has a conscience, a conscience informed by Scripture and subject to God. And the Christian believer knows that, apart from the convictions of the church of God in every age, and apart also from the present evidence that human life can have its beginning only at one point – the Christian knows that God became man in Jesus Christ. Not in his first breathing the air of Bethlehem, not in his becoming 'viable' some weeks before his mother's arrival in royal David's city, not at 'quickening', or 'animation', nor by gradations during the middle weeks of gestation, but Jesus Christ was *conceived by the Virgin Mary*, when the Holy Spirit 'came upon' her, and the power of the Most High 'overshadowed' her. That is when he took our humanity to himself, so that is when our humanity begins.

And Scripture bears abundant witness to this, as many times the continuity of life before and after birth is spelt out. So when it is asked whether the Bible condemns abortion, the answer is plain. The Ten Commandments decree that innocent human life is sacred, and (as the ancient Jews and the first Christians plainly said) there is no exception for the unborn (to permit abortion) any more than for the newly-born (to permit that other common practice, infanticide). Science and Scripture join in pointing to the moment of fertilization as the beginning of human life in the image of God.

SO WHAT CAN WE DO?

The Christian who sees abortion as it has been set out in these pages – as the destruction of a human life without just cause – will find it difficult to avoid the question of his or her own response. The Christian conscience, once awakened, will not sleep.

For doctors, nurses, social workers and others whose professional life involves them directly in decisions about abortion, the problems can be considerable (we have discussed them above), but there are many opportunities for a clear testimony against this great evil.

For others it may not be so plain. Yet there is something for every Christian to do. There are, of course, great organizations which have pitted themselves to political action, for it is only by such action that the law can be changed. Some will feel themselves called into active membership, perhaps into leadership, of these societies. Many more will wish to associate with them by giving to them and supporting them when occasion arises. Those who are in leadership in the churches bear a special burden of responsibility, since it was to a large degree the churches' failure to act twenty years ago which permitted the passage of the 1967 Act with such ease. At every level – congregational and national – the churches of Jesus Christ must make public their stand on this matter. Abortion, as one of the greatest evils of the century, must be the subject of preaching and teaching, and Christians in medicine, politics, the social services and wherever they have opportunity should bare their consciences and plead the cause of the innocent unborn.

There is ground to be made up, and the equivocation of the Protestant churches in years past requires atonement in the present. It must begin with prayer: prayer for forgiveness for us for our silence; prayer for forgiveness for others – so many others, and especially doctors and mothers – for their actions; prayer for the nation, that it will turn back from this dreadful course on which it has embarked. And it will be prayer in the name of Jesus, who was once a little child in Mary's womb; Jesus, whose young life was so terribly threatened; Jesus, the friend of the deformed and the unlovely, and the forgiver of sinners.

Notes

Chapter 1. WHAT DOES THE BIBLE SAY?

[1]Middle Assyrian Law 53.

[2]M. J. Gorman, *Abortion and the Early Church* (Downers Grove, USA, 1982), p.33.

[3]*Ibid.*, p.34.

[4]*Against Apion* ii.202, cited in G. J. Wenham, 'A Biblical theologian looks at Abortion', in *Abortion. The Biblical and Medical Challenges* (London, 1983).

[5]Cited in G. J. Wenham, *op. cit.*

[6]The text in Exodus 21 which is often brought up in discussions of abortion (though it is not concerned with this subject) is the subject of Appendix 2, below.

[7]The condemnation of *pharmakeia* in Galatians 5:20 and Revelation 18:23, and *pharmakoi* in Revelation 9:21; 21:8 and 22:15, is thought by many to include the abortifacient drugs and their purveyors. But a case cannot be built with certainty on these texts.

[8]We are not seeking to dramatize the discussion by using the word 'murder', simply to identify the biblical position. Murder (homicide might be a better word) is the deliberate killing of a human being without just cause (in Scripture, such causes are limited to two: the fighting of a just war, and execution – capital punishment). The Bible, like modern systems of law, recognizes the mitigating significance of motive and circumstance, so we do not suggest that the guilt of the abortionist or his collaborator is necessarily akin to that of a 'murderer'. Apart from anything else, he (or she) may not think that the fetus to be killed is a human being. But it is not possible to pursue this discussion with clarity unless spades are called by their proper names. We intend no offence to those who conscientiously disagree with us, but the entire argument turns on the nature of the unborn child, and if the sixth commandment covers him and her, then abortion is forbidden as, precisely, 'a special case of murder'.

[9]Some recent writers have called this 'speciesism'. By this they

mean that the belief that man is special *just because he is man* is arbitrary and wrong. In this wrongness 'speciesism' has an analogy with 'racism'. This is a profoundly pagan idea, since the Bible is absolutely plain that the specialness of man lies precisely in his being man, the only creature made in the divine image. This arises out of a morality based on evolution, and is related to extremist notions of 'animal liberation', which seek to put animals on the same level as man, a curious inversion of the older evolutionism which put man on the same level as the animals. Either way (and whether or not we accept organic evolution) the Bible makes the distinction very clear. Man is so special that he who kills him forfeits his own life, since he has killed the bearer of the image of God. Man's real responsibilities in his use of nature are of a different order.

[10]This argument from 'begetting' could be developed further, as in the following: 'The view that human life begins at fertilisation is in full accord with the Biblical data. It is supported in particular by the repeated emphasis that fathers beget (or generate) children. It is obvious that the father plays no part in the implantation, the embryonic development or the birth of his child. What he does contribute is half of the necessary genetic material at fertilisation. Thus the begetting of the child is identical with fertilisation, and the life of the child must begin then.' A. J. McDonald in the *Free Church Monthly Record*, January 1985.

[11]We discuss this theory below, in chapter 7.

[12]It would be possible to read Elizabeth's greeting proleptically, as meaning 'the one who *will be* the mother of my Lord'. But this is a less likely reading, since Elizabeth believed her own unborn child to have 'leaped for joy', 'filled with the Holy Spirit' (Luke 1:15). Mary's child, with his so much greater significance, can hardly be thought by her to be less significant *in utero* than her own.

[13]The idea that the 'soul' enters the fetus at some later stage is not a biblical doctrine, and indeed the notion of the 'soul' as a separate entity which is added to the physical body of man by God is distinctly unbiblical in origin. The whole subject is discussed by J. W. Montgomery in his essay 'The Christian View of the Fetus' in *Birth Control and the Christian*, ed. W. O. Spitzer and C. L. Saylor (Wheaton, Ill., 1969). The nature of man is supremely demonstrated in the manhood of Jesus Christ, and the narrative of the incarnation itself shows here the impossibility of an 'ensoulment' doctrine.

The attempt, sometimes made, to connect the 'ensoulment' of man with Genesis 2:7, 'man became a living soul', is naive, since in Hebrew the word *nephesh* is used also of animals and is never used of the spirit of man after death. It simply does *not* mean what some Christians mean by 'soul', and nor does any other biblical word.

[14]That the incarnation took place in Mary's womb is, interest-

128

ingly, openly accepted by Gareth Jones in the second edition of his book *Brave New People* (chapter 7). He writes: 'Even the life of the Son of God was, for nine months, enshrined in the life of a fetus.' This makes his defence of abortion (although it is highly qualified) all the more strange. See chapter 7, below.

Chapter 2. THE CHURCH'S VIEW

[1]Indeed, both the Church of England and the Church of Scotland have urged amending or reviewing the 1967 Abortion Act. The General Synod of the Church of England, in July 1983, passed this motion:
'That this Synod:
(a) believes that all human life including life developing in the womb, is created by God in His own image and is, therefore, to be nurtured, supported and protected;
(b) views with serious concern the number and consequences of abortions performed in the United Kingdom in recent years;
(c) recognises that in situations where the continuance of a pregnancy threatens the life of the mother a termination of pregnancy may be justified and that there must be adequate and safe provision in our society for such situations;
(d) commends to church members the work of those societies and agencies of the church that counsel and care for mothers and their babies;
(e) reaffirms the principles expressed in its resolutions of February 1974 and July 1975 which drew attention to the need to amend the Abortion Act 1967 and urges the Government to give priority to doing so.'
The General Assembly of the Church of Scotland, in May 1985, passed this deliverance:
'The General Assembly . . .
17. Receive the report on abortion and, reaffirming that on Biblical and historic Christian conviction the foetus is from the beginning an independent human being, conclude that its inviolability can be threatened only in the case of risk to maternal life, and that after the exhaustion of all alternatives.
18. Are aware of the ethical issues, the hard moral choices, and the pain felt by all involved in cases of pregnancy termination, and ask the Church to support with compassion those in this situation.
19. Urge local congregations to provide within a caring community a healthy and welcoming environment and counselling facilities for young people.
20. Commit the Church to securing a review of the 1967 Abortion Act.'
[2]R. F. R. Gardner, *Abortion: the Personal Dilemma* (Exeter, 1972), p.98.

[3]Art. 'Fœticide' in Hastings' *Encyclopaedia of Religion and Ethics* (Edinburgh, 1913), vol. vi.

[4]*Metamorphoses* 8, cited in M. J. Gorman, *Abortion and the Early Church*, p.28.

[5]*Art. cit.*

[6]M. J. Gorman, *op. cit.*, pp.15–17, citing Tertullian, *De Anima* 25. Square brackets Gorman's.

[7]M. J. Gorman, *op. cit.*, pp.33f.

[8]*Ibid.*, p.45.

[9]Hastings' *Encyclopaedia of Religion and Ethics*, *art. cit.*

[10]David Braine, *Medical Ethics and Human Life* (Aberdeen, 1982), pp.11f. We are indebted to Dr Braine, and his collaborator Mr Anthony Schmitz, for kind and ready permission to use patristic material collected in this valuable essay, where full references to the above citations may be found.

[11]Cited in Hastings' *Encyclopaedia of Religion and Ethics*, *art. cit.*

[12]Augustine, *De Civitate Dei* xxii.13.

[13]David Braine, *op. cit.*, pp.11f.

Chapter 3. THE LAW

[1]Figure derived from R. F. R. Gardner, *Abortion: the Personal Dilemma*, p.32 – a compilation of NHS and P. Diggory's figures.

[2]Appendix 1, Abortion Statistics, Table 1.

[3]Gerard Wright, QC, 'The Legal Implications of IVF', chapter 5 of *Test Tube Babies – a Christian View* (London/Oxford, 1984), p.43.

[4]T. G. A. Bowles and M. N. M. Bell, 'Abortion – a clarification', *New Law Journal*, 27 September 1979.

[5]G. Wright, *op. cit.*, p.42.

[6]Luton gynaecologist, Mr A. J. Hamilton, was accused of attempted murder of a baby boy born as a result of a prostaglandin termination. The gestation was mistaken and the child survived despite being bundled off to the sluice. Mr Hamilton was acquitted and reinstated to his post.

[7]For SPUC and other pro-life organizations – see Appendix 3.

[8]R. F. R. Gardner, *op. cit.*, p.59.

[9]The reader is particularly referred to Note 16 of the next chapter.

[10]T. G. A. Bowles and M. N. M. Bell, 'Abortion on Demand or on Request: Is it Legal?', The Law Society's *Guardian Gazette*, 24 September 1980.

[11]Appendix 1, Abortion Statistics, Table 4.

[12]David Field, 'The Question of Abortion', *Care Trust News*, No.7, October/November 1984, p.10.

[13]Organizations such as LIFE, with legal advice, have composed a standard letter which is suitable for nurses, *etc.*, to send to their administrators.

[14]T. G. A. Bowles and M. N. M. Bell, 'Abortion – a Clarification'.

[15]The Lane Report, *Report of the Committee on the Working of the Abortion Act; Survey of Abortion Patients* (HMSO, 1974).

[16]Ronald Reagan, *Abortion and the Conscience of the Nation* (Nashville, Tennessee, 1984), p.36.

Chapter 4. ABORTION IN PRACTICE

[1]This tragedy is further discussed in chapter 8, pp.108ff.

[2]*Family Planning Handbook for Doctors* (International Planned Parenthood Federation, London, 1980 edition), p.61.

[3]Wendy Savage and Irene Paterson, 'Abortion: methods and sequelae'. *British Journal of Hospital Medicine*, October 1982, p.364.

[4]Appendix 1, Abortion Statistics, Table 5.

[5]Appendix 1, Abortion Statistics, Tables 4 and 6.

[6]Appendix 1, Abortion Statistics, Table 3.

[7]Appendix 1, Abortion Statistics, Table 7.

[8]This whole area has been of concern to the medical profession and the subject of a recent study by the Royal College of Obstetricians and Gynaecologists, *Late Abortions in England and Wales, Report of a National Confidential Study*, edited by Professor Eva Alberman and Professor K. J. Dennis (RCOG, London, 1984).

[9]Luton gynaecologist, Mr Anthony J. Hamilton, was accused of attempted murder of a baby born as a late abortion. The gestational age was mistaken by a wide margin. Mr Hamilton's name was cleared in 1983 and he continues in practice as a hospital consultant.

[10]Antenatal screening is highly topical. For the interested reader the following publications provide amplification.
Prenatal Diagnosis, Proceedings of the Eleventh Study Group of the Royal College of Obstetricians and Gynaecologists, edited by C. H. Rodeck and K. H. Nicolaides (RCOG, London, 1984) (a technical volume!).

D. J. H. Brock, *Early Diagnosis of Fetal Defects*, Current Reviews in Obstetrics and Gynaecology (Edinburgh, 1982) (very readable).

[11]These figures are derived from the above publications.

[12]*Report of the RCOG working party on routine ultrasound examination in pregnancy* (RCOG, London, 1984).

[13]'Induced abortion operations and their early sequelae', Joint study of the Royal College of General Practitioners and the Royal College of Obstetricians and Gynaecologists, *Journal of the Royal College of General Practitioners*, April 1985, pp. 175–180.

P.I. Frank, C. R. Kay, T. L. T. Lewis and S. Parish, 'Outcome of pregnancy following induced abortion', Report from the joint study of the Royal College of General Practitioners and the Royal College of Obstetricians and Gynaecologists, *British Journal of Obstetrics and Gynaecology*, April 1985, pp.308–316.

[14]J. K. Russell, *Early Teenage Pregnancy*, Current Reviews in

Obstetrics and Gynaecology (Edinburgh, 1982), p.18. 'My experience is that the cervix is particularly vulnerable to dilatation and in spite of all the care, the small, immature cervix of a girl aged 13 to 16 is especially liable to be damaged in the course of legal termination of pregnancy. Laceration of the cervix is more likely and I suspect that these youngsters are more liable to suffer physiological as well as anatomical damage to the cervix.' (retired Professor of Obstetrics and Gynaecology, University of Newcastle-upon-Tyne).

[15]Several reports in the medical literature confirm this, for example, G. L. Ridgway, G. Mumtaz, R. A. Stephens and J. D. Oriel, 'Therapeutic abortion and chlamydial infection', *British Medical Journal*, vol. 286, 7 May 1983, p.1478.

[16]Pregnancy-related deaths, from whatever cause, are thoroughly examined and the results published in a report which covers a three year period. The numbers are relatively small so more frequent publication would be unhelpful. The reader interested in a comprehensive breakdown of deaths associated with abortion is referred to the latest (at the time of writing) *Report on Confidential Enquiries into Maternal Deaths in England and Wales, 1976–1978* (HMSO, London, 1982). Suffice it to say here that a total of 227 women died during that triennium of causes directly attributable to the pregnancy, of those, 19 died having abortions (spontaneous and induced). Of the abortion deaths 5 were due to anaesthetic complications. Table 8 of Appendix 1 shows the trend over the years.

Those who argue that it is safer to have an abortion than a full-term pregnancy use the figures to show that the Maternal Mortality Rate is around 130 per 1,000,000 *births* (including abortion deaths), whereas for legal abortion there are about 30 deaths per 1,000,000 *operations*. We answered this line of reasoning in the last chapter.

[17]Wendy Savage and Irene Paterson, 'Abortion: methods and sequelae', *British Journal of Hospital Medicine*, October 1982.

Chapter 5. THE AFTERMATH

[1]Appendix 1, Abortion Statistics, Table 8.
[2]*Legalised Abortion* (RCOG, London, 1966).
[3]R. H. S. Crossman, *New Statesman*, 7 August 1970, p.138; also note Appendix 1, Abortion Statistics, Table 8.
[4]R. F. R. Gardner, *Abortion: the Personal Dilemma*, p.42.
[5]F. A. Schaeffer and C. E. Koop, *Whatever Happened to the Human Race?* (London, 1980), p.17.
[6]P. G. Ney, 'Infant Abortion and Child Abuse: Cause and Effect', in *The Psychological Aspects of Abortion*, ed. D. Mall and W. F. Watts (Washington D. C., 1979), p.26.
We quote:

'1) Abortion decreases an individual's instinctual restraint against the occasional rage felt toward those dependent on his or her care.

2) Permissive abortion diminishes the social taboo against aggressing the defenceless.

3) Abortion increases the hostility between the generations. (Born children wonder if they were wanted.)

4) Abortion has devalued children, thus diminishing the value of caring for children. (Older children sense this – hence the rising suicide rate in young people.)

5) Abortion increases guilt and self-hatred, which the parent takes out on the child. (There is in addition what has been termed the 'survivor syndrome' in other children of the family – manifesting in aggression.)

6) Abortion increases hostility between the sexes – men are threatened by 'Women's Lib', and women are bitter towards men, who having impregnated them, pressurise into abortion. (Battered-wives often co-exist with battered-children.)

7) Abortion truncates the developing mother-infant bond, thereby diminishing her future mothering capability.'

[7] F. A. Schaeffer and C. E. Koop, *Whatever Happened to the Human Race?* p.46.

[8] Appendix 1, Abortion Statistics, Table 9.

[9] Appendix 1, Abortion Statistics, Table 10.

[10] Appendix 1, Abortion Statistics, Table 11.

[11] We have already referred to J. K. Russell, *Early Teenage Pregnancy*, Current Reviews in Obstetrics and Gynaecology, in the last chapter, Note 14. He comments that young girls do not use contraception properly and their availability simply leads to increasing levels of sexual activity (see chapter 5). Would that some of Professor Russell's sentiments were taken to heart by the medical profession! 'Moral leadership is urgently required but there is scant reference to this need in the literature . . . I am critical of the present strong undertone of contempt for standards and values which have long bound families together and have contributed to the stability of our society – discipline, truth, service to the community, gentleness and consideration for others, a sense of responsibility and chastity before and fidelity after marriage.' (pp.52–53).

[12] Appendix 1, Abortion Statistics, Table 12.

[13] 'Population arguments' are commonly thrown into discussions on abortion. On this complex topic Michael N. M. Bell's article in the news-sheet of the Association of Lawyers for the Defence of the Unborn, Number 23, Autumn 1984, is recommended. We would also recommend Germaine Greer's *Sex and Destiny – the Politics of Human Fertility* (London, 1984) to anyone with a special interest in political and anthropological details relevant to population. Others

have argued that abortion does not in fact affect the birthrate (see Richard Sherlock, 'The Demographic Argument for Liberal Abortion Policies; Analysis of a Pseudo-Argument', in T. W. Hilgers, D. J. Horan and D. Mall, editors, *New Perspectives in Human Abortion*, Frederick, Maryland, 1981, pp.450–465).

[14]Appendix 1, Abortion Statistics, Tables 4 and 6.

[15]M. H. Liebman and J. S. Zimmer, 'The Psychological Sequelae of Abortion: Fact and Fallacy', in *The Psychological Aspects of Abortion*, pp.127ff.

[16]M. Sim and R. Neisser, 'Post-Abortive Psychoses: a Report from Two Centers', in *The Psychological Aspects of Abortion*, pp.1ff.

[17]J. F. Murphy and K. O'Driscoll, 'Therapeutic Abortion: The Medical Argument', *Irish Medical Journal*, August 1982, vol. 75, pp.304ff.

[18]M. Sim and R. Neisser, *op. cit.*, p.12. Dr Sim concludes that 'abortion has no place in the treatment of the mentally ill or, for that matter, in the prevention of mental illness'.

[19]This view is expressed by Professor Gordon Stirrat in *Legalised Abortion – the Continuing Dilemma* (London, 1979).

[20]R. F. R. Gardner, *Abortion: the Personal Dilemma*, p.51.

[21]Appendix 1, Abortion Statistics, note footnote of Table 3.

[22]R. F. R. Gardner, *Abortion: the Personal Dilemma*, p.51. See also Note 13 of chapter 3.

Chapter 6. THE LIFE OF THE UNBORN

[1]Oliver O'Donovan, *The Christian and the Unborn Child*, Grove Booklet on Ethics No.1 (Nottingham, 1980); pp. 12 and 13 are particularly helpful.

[2]The term 'clone' used more scientifically applies to cell lines. In very early development (4 to 8 cell stage) each cell has the capacity to become any cell in the body (totipotency). Differentiation, causing different types of tissue to form, is achieved by genes 'switching on' or 'off'. Many generations of different types of cell are produced.

[3]Lennart Nilsson, *A Child is Born* (London, 1977), p.50.

[4]Thomas Verny, MD, with John Kelly, *The Secret Life of the Unborn Child* (London, 1982).

Chapter 7. DEFENDING ABORTION

[1]Leicester, 1984. Now republished in a second edition in the USA by William B. Eerdmans (1985).

[2]*Brave New People*, pp.162ff.

[3]For an argument that does use this category, see Oliver O'Donovan, *Begotten or Made?* (Oxford, 1984), chapter 4. This book, though not easy reading, is a most important contribution to dis-

cussion. Professor O'Donovan holds the Regius Chair of Moral and Pastoral Theology at Oxford.

[4]T. F. Torrance, *Test-tube Babies* (Edinburgh, 1984). This short booklet represents a major statement by one of the world's leading thinkers about the relations of science and religion.

[5]Professor Jones's ready acceptance, clearer in the US second edition of his book, of much of the theological and biblical analysis which we have presented above, makes his conclusions the more difficult to accept. The prominence of this book in recent controversy in the USA, where he has been labelled 'pro-abortion', has not taken account of his deep and plain unhappiness with every abortion. His arguments and his instincts seem, alike, to be against it. But the door is left ajar for the exceptional case of serious genetic disorder, where the logic is that of the termination of the life of the severely disabled. This is, from a Hippocratic and a Christian perspective, compassion that has gone seriously astray. The door remains open also for abortion after rape, and Jones suggests (somewhat prejudicially) that the issue is 'whether a woman should be allowed to be treated as anything other than as a fully human person', whether she 'should be forced to be a mother against her will'. But if she has become pregnant through rape she has *already* been 'forced to be a mother against her will'. Professor Jones's question-begging terminology is less than helpful here, and his compassion leads him to imply that those who respect the fetus as well as the mother are lacking in compassion. Their compassion is informed by another, and a more rigorous, ethical analysis. Professor Jones's 'compassion' denies the biblical ontology of the fetus which he has earlier accepted.

[6]*Abortion: the Personal Dilemma* (Exeter, 1972), p.126.

[7]*Ibid.*, p.124; citing James Barr.

[8]*Ibid.*, p.123.

[9]*Ibid.*, p.123.

[10]*Ibid.*, p.124. We turn to some discussion of the present issues of *in vitro* technology in chapter 9, below.

[11]*Ibid.*, p.131.

[12]*Ibid.*, p.140.

[13]London, 1979.

[14]*Legalised Abortion*, p.29.

[15]Nottingham, 1973.

[16]*The Christian and the Unborn Child*, p.19.

[17]*By What Standard?* (London, 1977).

Chapter 8. HARD QUESTIONS

[1]*De Civitate Dei* xxii.13.

Chapter 9. ALL OUR TOMORROWS

[1]An important discussion of the nature of the embryo, bringing insights from biology and genetics to bear on a philosophical analysis, is to be found in an article by Teresa Iglesias, 'What Kind of Being is the Human Embryo?' in *Ethics and Medicine* 2:1, 1986.

[2]Few people realize that, already, human fetuses have been used for laboratory vivisection. They are not covered by the legislation which protects animals and requires the issuing of a licence from the Home Office before an experiment can take place. An example of this horrific practice is as follows. Professor M. C. Macnaughton, a distinguished gynaecologist who is currently (1985) President of the Royal College of Obstetricians and Gynaecologists and was a member of the Warnock Committee, in the late 1960s published two papers in the *Journal of Endocrinology* in which he and a colleague reported on experiments of this kind. They had obtained fetuses of up to 22 weeks' gestation after abortions and kept them alive for up to two hours, during which time they were exposed to radio-activity and after which they were dissected and their organs ground with sand in a pestle and mortar. When the public is being assured that the 14-day limit recommended by the Warnock Committee will be adhered to, and that later embryos will never be used for experiment, the past record of the President of the Royal College needs to be remembered. (*Journal of Endocrinology* 39, pp. 153–162; 44, pp.481–488.)

[3]Sir Peter Tizard and Dr T. L. Chambers wrote: 'We agree [with Dr Cameron's letter of May 29th, 1984] with the implication that there is no ethical distinction to be drawn between the killing of a foetus and of a new-born baby.' It is interesting that their denial of infanticide on the part of their colleagues was qualified. They 'do not countenance the deliberate killing of a deformed new-born baby who, *with ordinary care*, would survive' (our emphasis). They are not speaking about babies who would require something more than that. Letter, *The Times*, 1 June 1984.

[4]F. A. Schaeffer and C. E. Koop, in their book *Whatever Happened to the Human Race?* (London, 1980), quote Nobel prize-winners Crick and Watson to this effect, and give references to ethicists and others who have echoed the same sentiments, pp.53ff.

Appendix 1
Abortion statistics

We are indebted to Professor J. J. Scarisbrick, Honorary Chairman of LIFE, for his permission to reproduce, with certain modifications, the following tables (with the exception of Tables 2 and 8). The statistics have been derived from publications of the Office of Population Censuses and Surveys - *Abortion Statistics*, *Population Trends*, *Monitors*, and *Annual Abstract of Statistics*.

Table 1
ABORTION: annual totals for England and Wales

	1977	1979	1981	1982	1983
Total	133,004	149,746	162,480	163,045	162,161
Resident	102,677	120,611	128,581	128,553	127,375
Non-resident	30,327	29,135	33,899	34,492	34,786

(two thirds of non-residents were Spanish women by 1981)

Table 2
ABORTION: some US figures
(as supplied by United States Information Service, US Embassy)
Legal abortions, by selected characteristics: 1973 to 1980
[Number of abortions from surveys conducted by source; characteristics from the U.S. Centers for Disease Control's (CDC) annual abortion surveillance summaries, with adjustments for changes in States reporting data to the CDC each year]

Characteristic	Number (1,000)							
	1973	1974	1975	1976	1977	1978	1979	1980
Total legal abortions	744·6	898·6	1,034·2	1,179·3	1,316·7	1,409·6	1,497·7	1,553·9
Age of woman:								
Less than 15 years old	11·6	13·4	15·3	15·8	15·7	15·1	16·2	15·3
15–19 years old	232·4	278·3	324·9	362·7	396·6	418·8	444·6	444·8
20–24 years old	240·6	286·6	331·6	392·3	449·7	489·4	525·7	549·4
25–29 years old	129·6	162·7	188·9	220·5	246·7	266·0	284·2	303·8
30–34 years old	72·6	89·8	100·2	110·1	124·4	134·3	142·0	153·1
35–39 years old	41·0	48·8	52·7	56·7	61·7	65·3	65·1	66·6
40 years old and over	16·8	19·0	20·5	21·3	22·0	20·7	19·9	20·9
Race of woman:								
White	548·8	629·3	701·2	784·9	888·8	969·4	1,062·4	1,093·6
Black and other	195·8	269·3	333·0	394·4	427·9	440·2	435·3	460·3
Marital status of woman:								
Married	216·2	248·2	271·9	290·0	299·7	350·6	322·2	319·9
Unmarried	528·4	650·4	762·3	889·3	1,017·0	1,059·0	1,175·5	1,234·0
Number of prior live births:								
None	375·2	482·5	499·3	562·6	742·5	798·1	868·2	900·0
1	137·4	155·5	206·8	244·4	249·4	271·3	287·1	304·8
2	102·2	130·1	156·8	181·5	186·5	198·0	207·0	215·6
3	61·7	70·3	86·8	97·7	80·0	83·3	82·1	82·9
4 or more	68·2	60·2	84·4	93·1	58·4	58·9	53·3	50·6
Number of prior induced abortions:								
None	(NA)	762·1	822·1	911·3	966·7	994·5	1,023·3	1,040·8
1	(NA)	112·6	170·4	213·2	267·8	315·5	350·4	371·0
2 or 3	(NA)	24·0	41·7	54·7	82·2	99·6	124·0	142·1
Weeks of gestation:								
Less than 9 weeks	284·3	399·4	480·6	559·9	657·9	707·8	748·5	800·0
9–10 weeks	221·6	256·5	290·4	333·8	361·2	388·4	412·9	416·5
11–12 weeks	130·6	134·9	151·1	171·3	179·5	187·7	203·6	201·8
13 weeks or more	108·2	107·8	112·1	114·4	118·2	125·7	132·6	135·7

Table 2 (continued)
ABORTION: some US figures
Legal abortions, estimated number, rate and ratio: 1973 to 1980
(refers to women 15–44 years old at time of abortion)

	1973	1974	1975	1976	1977	1978	1979	1980
Women, 15–44 years old (1,000)	45,590	46,608	47,606	48,721	49,814	50,920	52,016	53,048
Number of abortions (1,000)	744·6	898·6	1,034·2	1,179·3	1,316·7	1,409·6	1,497·7	1,553·9
Rate per 1,000 women	16·3	19·3	21·7	24·2	26·4	27·7	28·8	29·3
Ratio per 1,000 live births	239	282	331	361	400	417	422	428

Table 3
ABORTION: residents and non-residents by place of abortion

	Total	Residents NHS hospitals	Residents private clinics	Non-residents NHS hospitals	Non-residents private clinics
1968	23,641	14,492	7,840	68	1,241
1970	86,565	47,370	28,592	308	10,295
1972	159,884	56,861	51,704	225	51,094
1974	162,940	56,076	53,369	244	53,251
1976	129,673	50,569	51,343	205	27,556
1978	141,558	55,040	56,811	207	29,500
1979	149,746	55,558	65,053	209	28,926
1980	160,903	60,594	68,333	224	31,752
1981	162,480	61,103	67,478	173	33,726
1982	163,045	62,409	66,144*	123	34,369
1983	162,161	62,609	64,766*	208	34,578

*includes over 4,000 abortions done under agency agreements

Table 4

ABORTION: residents and non-residents, by statutory grounds*

	Grounds*						4 with	
	1	2	3	4	5	6	2 &/or 3	3 with 2
1974	4,146	131,126	3,101	972	3	6	975	22,601
1976	2,061	110,504	2,535	661	1	9	769	13,133
1978	2,124	118,671	2,492	1,442	5	7	1,129	15,688
1979	1,036	128,726	2,092	1,321	3	10	1,086	15,472
1980	702	140,491	1,961	1,031	4	3	1,008	15,703
1981	790	158,520	20,713	2,053	5	9	—	—
1982	674	159,418	17,796	2,282	7	5	—	—
1983	549	158,389	18,098	2,268	3	3	—	—

Note that from 1981 the number of 'mentions' are given – in about 10% of abortions more than one ground is listed.

*Statutory grounds
1. risk to mother's life
2. risk of injury to the mother's physical or mental health
3. risk of injury to the physical or mental health of existing born children
4. substantial risk of serious handicap (of the child)
5. in an emergency to save the mother's life
6. in an emergency to prevent grave permanent injury to the mother

Table 5

ABORTION: gestational age in weeks (residents and non-residents)

	Under 9	9–12	13–16	17–19	20–23	24 and over	not stated
1974	39,174	87,623	25,506	4,438	1,509	199	4,491
1976	31,494	68,994	18,801	4,146	1,715	218	4,305
1978	33,222	76,426	19,823	4,669	2,262	359	4,797
1979	35,273	80,676	20,771	5,164	2,453	438	4,671
1980	37,197	86,255	22,792	5,893	3,040	613	5,113
				17–20	21–24	25 and over	Unknown
1981	48,724	83,415	19,384	7,563	2,062	142	1,164
1982	51,692	82,519	18,382	7,945	2,314	102	91
1983	53,950	79,325	18,520	7,713	2,446	97	110

Table 6
ABORTION: 1983 medical conditions (residents only)

	Total	This as % of all abortions done*
Mother's condition: physical *e.g.* diabetes and hypertension	1,210	0.95
Mother's condition: mental (total)	112,901	88.6
e.g. non-serious – neurotic and 'depressive'	(111,879)	(87.8)
Child's condition: known or suspected *e.g.* central nervous system disorder and chromosomal abnormality	2,235	1.75
No mention of any medical condition	10,908	8.56

*i.e. the totals of principal medical conditions mentioned as
percentage of the 127,375 abortions performed on
residents in 1983. Only about 1,400 other mentions of
medical conditions are recorded. Thus in 99% of
cases the 'principal medical condition' is the only one
mentioned.

Table 7
*ABORTION: methods used, NHS and non-NHS premises
(residents and non-residents)*

	surgery*	vacuum aspiration	D&C	D&C and aspiration	prosta-glandin	saline	not stated
1971	12,482	52,767	57,731	‡	‡	‡	207
1975	2,740	99,218	18,638	20,476	8,037	1,073	428
1977	1,560	85,702	14,678	20,705	8,483	1,387	263
1979	1,125	103,776	9,963	22,825	9,607	2,101	319
1980	909	108,649	11,837	27,106	10,295	1,831	235
1981	767	109,593	8,189	32,447	10,051		
1982	511	112,370	5,608	33,062	10,058		
1983	493	106,818	6,097	37,103	11,609		

*hysterotomy and hysterectomy, only and with others
‡figure not available

Table 8

ABORTION DEATHS in triennial reports 1952–78, by type of abortion with estimated rates per million maternities and the estimated rates per million conceptions, 1970–78 (excluding anaesthetic deaths)

Type of abortion	1952–1954	1955–1957	1958–1960	1961–1963	1964–1966	1967–1969	1970–1972	1973–1975	1976–1978
Illegal	108	91	82	77	98	74	38	10	4
Spontaneous	43	50	52	57	25	25	6	5	2
Legal	2	—	1	5	10	18	37	14	8
Totals	153	141	135	139	133	117	81	29	14
Rates per million maternities	74·5	66·7	58·8	55·1	51·1	47·6	35·2	15·1	7·4
Rate per million conceptions	—	—	—	—	—	—	29·1	11·9	6·2

(Report on Confidential Enquiries into Maternal Deaths in England and Wales 1976–1978, HMSO, 1982, p.50)

Table 9
MALFORMED BORN BABIES:
congenital malformations, totals and rates (England and Wales)

	Total	overall rate*	Down's syndrome*	spina bifida*	central nervous system*	ear & eye*	heart*
1973	13,353	195·3	—	—	—	—	—
1975	12,230	200·6	7·4	18·1	36·5	6·1	10·2
1977	12,402	215·8	7·4	15·3	32·5	8·1	11·3
1979	13,529	210·4	7·3	13·1	25·5	6·8	12·0
1981	13,450	210·6	7·4	10·4	19·2	9·9	13·2
1982	13,281	210·9	8·4	8·1	16·1	11·3	13·9
1983	13,972	220·8	7·9	6·7	14·5	11·6	15·7

*rates per 10,000 total births

Table 10
BIRTHS, ILLEGITIMACY RATE AND DEATHS
(thousands)

	births	United Kingdom illegitimacy rate*	deaths
1961	944	5·7	632
1964	1,015	6·9	611
1967	962	8·1	617
1971	902	8·2	645
1974	737	8·7	667
1975	698	9·0	663
1976	676	9·0	681
1977	657	9·5	655
1978	687	10·0	667
1979	735	10·6	676
1980	754	11·5	662
1981	731	12·5	658
1982	719	14·1	663
1983	722	15·4	659
1984			

*rates per hundred live births

Table 11
ABORTION: mothers' age (residents only)

	Under 15	15	16–19	20–24	25–34	35–44
1969	326	852	8,059	12,914	16,982	9,248
1971	625	1,671	18,176	24,465	31,495	15,892
1974	845	2,490	24,197	26,561	36,403	16,795
1976	880	2,545	23,963	23,612	33,907	14,736
1978	844	2,454	26,363	26,693	37,097	16,071
1979	841	2,693	29,192	29,647	39,003	16,977
1980	933	2,717	31,878	33,014	41,461	18,037
1981	—	3,530*	31,381	34,266	40,632	17,627
1982	931	2,921	31,349	35,024	39,747	17,781
1983	1,029	3,058	31,231	35,014	39,060	17,454

*under 16. More detailed figures not available

Table 12
ABORTION: previous live born children (residents only)

	Number of previous children					
	0	1	2	3	4	5 and over
1971	43,413	10,383	16,307	12,092	6,506	4,269
1974	53,545	13,405	20,400	12,550	5,746	3,691
1976	50,826	12,572	18,962	10,745	4,591	2,733
1978	57,998	14,532	21,239	10,976	4,197	2,312
1979	64,400	15,494	22,855	11,174	4,104	2,084
1980	70,232	16,664	23,927	11,426	4,194	2,159
1981	67,387	16,743	23,493	11,048	3,882	1,978
1982	69,296	17,041	23,369	10,554	3,666	1,832
1983	69,979	17,030	22,412	10,109	3,475	1,755

Appendix 2
A text in debate

There is one biblical text which frequently features in discussions of abortion. It is referred to by writers who believe abortion to be permissible, since they interpret it to teach that the life of the unborn child is of less value than the life of the child once born; and, therefore, that there is a difference in kind between life before and after birth. But the significance of this text for the debate rests on the claim which is often made that it is the only biblical reference that is relevant. As we have shown above, this is by no means the case. The nature of life before birth is evident at a number of key points in the 'birth narratives' at the beginning of the Gospel story, especially because these narratives are partly concerned with the birth of the supreme man, Jesus Christ. What is true of him as man must also be true of us, apart only from his sinlessness.

Exodus 21:22–25 is a law, part of the law code of the Pentateuch. It deals with the appropriate legal penalty in the (rather unusual) case of a fight between men which results in injury to a woman bystander who is pregnant. The meaning of the clauses in these verses is not entirely clear, but it is sufficiently clear to rule out any interpretation which would make induced abortion defensible. Apart from anything else, it is concerned with miscarriage induced *by accident*. No-one claims it is speaking about a deliberate attack on either the woman or her baby. It maintains two of the principles of moral responsibility in the Old Testament laws, and indeed of our laws today: a man is accountable for his actions, but less so if their consequences

are accidental. So manslaughter and murder are differenti-
ated in the Pentateuch, even as they are today.

According to Exodus 21, a fine is payable by the attacker
who accidentally injures the woman if she goes into premature labour as a result: 'When men strive together, and hurt
a woman with child, so that there is a miscarriage, and yet
no harm follows, the one who hurt her shall be fined . . .'
(RSV). On the other hand, 'If any harm follows', there will
be a reckoning of 'life for life' in the normal way.

This can be taken in one of two ways, depending on how
one answers the question, 'If any harm follows to whom?'
But neither of these interpretations leads to a result which
would support the practice of abortion.

One interpretation is to take both mother and child as
possible victims of 'harm'. That is, if the premature labour
results in a live birth, and mother and child do well with no
lasting injury, then the fine alone is adequate – it is simply a
penalty for recklessly causing the induction of labour. On
the other hand, if either mother or child is harmed – if the
child is too young to survive, or if some other injury has
permanent effects on either the mother or the baby – then
there will be a reckoning, 'life for life, eye for eye, tooth for
tooth, hand for hand, foot for foot, burn for burn, wound
for wound, stripe for stripe'.

The other interpretation leaves the child out of account.
'Harm' relates only to the mother. Whether the child survives the premature labour is not regarded as relevant, only
whether the mother is permanently injured as a result. On
this reading it is argued that the life of the child is regarded
as of much less significance than the life of the mother. The
taking of unborn life, therefore, is an option for us.

But this is by no means the case. Even assuming this
second interpretation to be the true one (and what we read
elsewhere in Scripture about the life of the unborn predis-
poses us to accept the first), we are not reading about a
punishment (or lack of it) for deliberately induced abortion;
it is intended to be punishment for an accidental consequence at two removes from the fight which is being
deliberately pursued. That is to say, the man concerned is
fighting another man. He may be reckless in doing so when
he is close to a bystander, but if she is struck or knocked
down it is not because he intended harm to her. She is

pregnant, and therefore her child may also be harmed, but the man may well not even know of her pregnancy. So his killing of the child, if the child dies, perhaps by reckless but light injury to the mother, is doubly unpremeditated.

Another consideration arises. The two verses immediately before the passage we are discussing are concerned with the punishment which is due if a master beats his slave to death. It is not our purpose here to enter into the complexities of the biblical view of slavery, but to make an altogether different point. The law related here provides that the master who beats to death his slave shall be 'punished', while if the man survives 'a day or two' he shall not be. Both of these penalties are very much less serious than would be their equivalent in the case of a non-slave. Scripture is not here discussing whether slaves are human beings; it is setting penalties for particular crimes. If we deduce from the penalty set in verse 22 that the unborn child is not a full human being, we have no option but to draw a similar conclusion here about the slave. In both cases it would be mistaken.

The other reading of verses 22–25 makes better sense, in any case. Either way, the passage cannot be taken to mean that the unborn child is less than a human being. Since it is concerned with accidental injury recklessly caused to the mother, and only by a double accident to the unborn child, it is hard to see how any comparison can be made with the morality of deliberate injury caused to the child to bring about its death, which is abortion.

A comment may be added on the use that is made of this passage by Rex Gardner in *Abortion: the Personal Dilemma*. Mr Gardner introduces the text with the assertion that it is the 'one clear reference to abortion in the Old Testament'. In doing so he is, of course, employing the term *abortion* in a technical sense to include accidental as well as induced abortion. Since throughout his book the term *abortion* is used of *induced, deliberate abortion*, it is misleading to imply that the Bible is here speaking of that same subject. The text is concerned not with what is generally referred to as abortion, but with miscarriage or (if the child survives) premature delivery.

Two or three different interpretations are introduced, and the author sums up his discussion in these terms: 'It would seem fairly obvious that in any case the text implies a difference in the eyes of the law between the fetus and a person' (p.119). Well, as we have suggested, it all depends how the passage is understood. And even if Mr Gardner's own understanding of it is followed and we do find here 'a difference in the eyes of the law between the fetus and a person', we must carefully qualify such a conclusion. For one thing, it is a difference in the eyes of the law in how punishment is decided in the case of a particular offence, in which (as we have seen) accidental injury is inflicted on a woman and/or her unborn child by the reckless brawling of two other individuals.

More important, the context must be borne in mind. A similar distinction to the one Mr Gardner finds in these verses is found a few verses earlier, and it lies between two parties, neither of whom Mr Gardner or the author of Exodus would regard as less than a 'person', a free man and a slave. In that case a difference in penalty for assaulting one or the other does not imply a difference in personal standing and nature. It arises, as we have suggested, for other reasons. So the notion that Scripture (a) discusses abortion and (b) in that context rules that there is a 'difference' between a 'fetus' and a 'person' (implying that the fetus cannot be a person) is seriously misleading, and it is regrettable that such a conclusion is built into the argument of *Abortion: the Personal Dilemma* from this point on.

Full discussions of the meaning of these verses may be found in *Law, Morality and the Bible*, ed. B. N. Kaye and G. J. Wenham (Leicester, 1978), pp.33f., where a number of references are to be found; and *Birth Control and the Christian*, ed. W. O. Spitzer and C. L. Saylor (Wheaton, Ill., 1969), pp.87ff.

Appendix 3
Further information

Reading

A considerable literature has grown up during the past twenty years addressing every aspect of the abortion question. Much of the best writing has, in our opinion, originated in North America, and a good deal of it from Roman Catholic writers.

A major collection of essays which will lead the enquirer to much else is *New Perspectives in Human Abortion*, edited by T. W. Hilgers, D. J. Horan and D. Mall (Frederick, Maryland, USA, 1981). A symposium from a distinctively biblical perspective is *Thou Shalt Not Kill*, edited by Richard L. Ganz (New York, 1978). Another wide-ranging collection (to which we have referred on a number of occasions) is *The Psychological Aspects of Abortion*, edited by D. Mall and W. F. Watts (Washington, D. C., 1979).

The most influential Christian volume on the subject to be published in Britain is R. F. R. Gardner's *Abortion: The Personal Dilemma* (Exeter, 1972), to which we have often referred and with which we have often disagreed. It is an informative book which has had great influence on evangelical Protestant thinking in the UK. Gareth Jones's *Brave New People* (Leicester, 1984) addresses the abortion issue in the context of debate about the new reproductive technology. We discuss both these books in chapter 7.

Oliver O'Donovan's booklet *The Christian and the Unborn Child* (Nottingham, 1973) remains the best short ethical analysis of the subject, and should be much more widely known. An important new symposium has just appeared, which includes contributions from Professor O'Donovan and others: *Abortion and the Sanctity of Human Life*, edited by J. H. Channer (Exeter, 1985).

Of great influence has been the book (and film series) entitled *Whatever Happened to the Human Race?* by the late Francis A. Schaeffer and Dr C. Everett Koop (London, 1980). Schaeffer and Koop link together abortion, infanticide and euthanasia as related consequences of abandoning the sanctity of human life.

A powerful statement against abortion at a popular level is John Powell's book *Abortion: The Silent Holocaust* (London, 1982).

Organizations
There are two main anti-abortion lobbies in the UK. LIFE sponsors caring as well as political work, while the *Society for the Protection of Unborn Children* concentrates on the latter. Other organizations with a major interest in the issue include CARE *Trust* and CARE *Campaigns* (the former Nationwide Festival of Light; an evangelical organization) and the *Order of Christian Unity*, an interdenominational grouping in which evangelicals are also involved. These all issue their own news magazines. *Rutherford House* in Edinburgh, through its *Medical Ethics Project*, organizes conferences on various issues on medical ethics and publishes a quarterly journal, *Ethics & Medicine*, which is read by doctors and also others concerned about this subject. The *World Federation of Doctors who Respect Human Life* is what it says, and has a British branch.

Addresses
LIFE, 118–120 Warwick Street, Leamington Spa, Warwickshire CV32 4QY

The Society for the Protection of Unborn Children (SPUC), 7 Tufton Street, London SW1P 3QN

CARE Trust and CARE Campaigns, 21A Down Street, London W1Y 7DN

The Order of Christian Unity, Christian Unity House, 58 Hanover Gardens, London SE11 5TN

Rutherford House Medical Ethics Project, Rutherford House, 17 Claremont Park, Edinburgh EH6 7PJ

The World Federation of Doctors Who Respect Human Life, 75 St Mary's Rd, Huyton, Merseyside L36 5SR

Index of biblical references

General index